THE VIKING SHIP

THE VIKING SHIP

BARBARA ANN CARLE

The Viking Ship
Copyright © 2018 by Barbara Ann Carle

ISBN: 978-0-9976261-2-4

Cover Designed by Carnes Group Creative
Copyedited and Formatted by D Tinker Editing

Published by Church Avenue Press
Houston, Texas

THE VIKING SHIP

When you were sick
you built a Viking ship
lovingly carved of white wood
It was intricate and beautiful

The dragon-headed prow
faced the future
Three hand-carved shields
decorated port and starboard

You fashioned tiny people
out of white paper
On long strips you wrote
thoughts and deeds
you wanted to set free
You rolled them up
tied them with twine
and placed them in the hull
I never read your scrolls

You planned a Viking funeral
to sail upon your favorite lake
set your ship afire
and release your worldly cares

In the hospital you said
Mom, don't forget to burn my ship.

Dearest Scott, please forgive me
After I lost you
I couldn't burn your ship
It is a part of you
I can't let go.

This book is dedicated to:

Ed, my beloved husband of fifty-eight years, who walked this path by my side and kept me strong.

My four children—Scott, Paula, Melissa, and Glen—who taught me infinite patience, the challenge of living in controlled chaos, and the joys of giving and receiving love.

Most of all, my son Scott, who fought the great fight with faith, grace, dignity, and yes, his own remarkable sense of humor.

Scott

Summer of 1992

INTRODUCTION

I had led a charmed life, right up until the day it wasn't.

"Mom, I have cancer."

Those four words took my breath away and catapulted my son and me on a journey that lasted less than two years. Scott, the oldest of my four children, was thirty-three years old. He had platinum-blond hair, just like his father—a gift of their German heritage—and clear blue eyes that grew dark and stormy whenever he became angry, which was seldom.

It was the evening of April 10, 1994. I had been surprised to see Scott and his wife, Carolyn, walk in my back door. We all lived in Nassau Bay, Texas, a small town directly across the street from the Johnson Space Center. Though they dropped by often, they rarely visited without their four children.

Scott and Carolyn had dated briefly during their senior year in high school. Several years later, they ran into each other at a restaurant in downtown Houston and began dating again. Carolyn had been divorced and was the mother of three small children: three-year-old Joshua and two-year-old twins, Sarah and Emily. When they announced they were getting married, Ed and I were delighted. Becoming instant grandparents was something we looked forward to.

They married in 1987, and in 1991, Carolyn and Scott had their first child, our granddaughter Rose.

A few months prior to the night Scott and Carolyn came to visit without their children, a mole on Scott's neck had darkened. His family physician had assured him there was nothing to worry about. He had felt the mole should be removed, though, since the collars of Scott's usual shirts would irritate it. Since it was located in a visible area, he suggested Scott see a plastic surgeon. This new doctor gave Scott the same assurance, but he also recommended the mole be biopsied as a precaution.

"Dr. Warner called this afternoon," Scott said when he and Carolyn came to visit. "It's melanoma."

Ed and I were stunned. Scott was six foot two and weighed almost two hundred pounds. He had never suffered a major illness or been hospitalized. He still had his tonsils, still had his appendix, and had never even broken a bone. How could he have cancer?

As we sat there on the couch, I covered his hand with mine and tried to reassure him. I named all the people I knew who had survived skin cancer. For just a moment, his eyes were touched with apprehension. Then he squeezed my hand and smiled. "Don't worry, Mom. I'll be fine."

Yet that night I felt the birth of fear and doubt.

For the previous seven years, Scott and Carolyn had been struggling to raise three children—and then four—on a teacher's salary. He had never intended to become a teacher. His first loves were art and photography. However, he had realized a career in fine arts could not support a family. After obtaining his bachelor's degree, he went on to obtain a master's degree in art education.

From his first day in the classroom, Scott realized he was a born teacher. He loved his students, and they loved him. But he eventually realized his future was in administration, and he had recently been named the youngest assistant principal in the history of the Pasadena, Texas, Independent School District. He loved working with the teenagers at Sam Rayburn High School, and the higher salary was making life easier for his family.

That night, after Scott and Carolyn left, I went to bed but couldn't sleep. After tossing and turning until two in the morning, I finally grabbed my pillow and headed for the family room.

I'd always loved that room. It was just large enough to fit three couches in a U-shaped configuration, with an extra-large coffee table in the middle. It was the perfect room for a family with four children, plus spouses, grandchildren, and all their friends. I lay down on the couch and covered myself with my mother's blue-and-white crocheted afghan. As I looked around the room, I thought that everything looked the same, yet nothing was the same. I could feel tiny tentacles of fear wrapping themselves around my chest.

They say when you depart this world, your life flashes before your eyes. As I lay huddled on that couch, the life that flashed before my eyes was Scott's.

JULY 23, 1960

That morning started out sweltering and muggy, typical for that time of year. Ed and I were spending the weekend at my parents' house in Queens, New York. We had just put a down payment on our first house out on Long Island. Of course, we had had no furniture, so my parents had given us their old maple living-room set. Ed was out on the back porch, refinishing the wood.

Since my due date was August 2nd, I hoped the baby would come a few days late and be born on August 5th, my birthday. I had been ignoring a nagging backache all morning and finally decided to go upstairs to take some aspirin.

"Why do you keep rubbing your back?" my mom asked. "Are you all right?"

I explained my distress, and she immediately told me to call my doctor. I was surprised when he said, "I'll meet you at the hospital within the hour."

Ed went into a mild panic, and I was reminded of the old *I Love Lucy* TV show, where Ricky rushes off in the car, leaving a poor pregnant Lucy behind. I watched him run around, ripping off his work clothes, throwing on clean slacks and a shirt, and all the while muttering, "Where are my keys? Do I need gas?"

I couldn't help laughing. Ed had never lost his keys; they were always in their designated spot. Gradually, he calmed down and drove me straight to Caledonian Hospital in Brooklyn.

The weather had been so hot that month that I was anxious for this pregnancy to be over, but at the same time, I was apprehensive. This was my first child, and I had heard all the horror stories: twenty-four-hour labors, C-sections. I made Ed promise that no matter how long it took, he would stay at the hospital. Fathers were not allowed in the labor or delivery rooms in those days, but I wanted to see Ed as soon as possible after the baby was born.

When we arrived at the hospital, they insisted I sit in a wheelchair while Ed filled out all the paperwork. I remember being rolled into the elevator and watching the doors close on Ed. He looked like he was watching them escort me to the electric chair.

I was all alone in the labor room. The hospitals weren't air-conditioned in those days. Fortunately, my bed was located next to the window, so a cool breeze occasionally drifted into the room.

When the doctor finally arrived, he said, "Boy, I had the devil of a time convincing your husband to go home. There's no point in him hanging around. A first baby can take hours. He and your mother would just be sitting downstairs all that time, and the chairs in the waiting room are really uncomfortable. Your mom and I finally talked him into leaving. I told him I'd call when it's close so he can get back in plenty of time to see you and the baby."

I smiled and agreed with the doctor, all the while thinking, *Oh, no, we wouldn't want Ed to be uncomfortable, would we?* So there I was, in labor for the first time and pissed at my husband.

And—surprise, surprise—my labor was only three hours short. My first child, Scott Edwin Carle, was born at 3:00 p.m. And of course, Ed was so far away, he arrived late. He felt terrible and looked terrible. But I was so happy that the minute I saw him, I forgave him.

Scott weighed nine and a half pounds and was twenty-three inches long. The day we brought him home from the hospital, we laid him on our big bed and unwrapped his blue receiving blanket. Ed performed the mandatory counting of fingers and toes and was happy to find everything in order. Scott laid there, kicking his long, spindly legs and trying to get his fist into his mouth. Ed and I fell madly in love with this child we had made.

Scott was the perfect first child. He had a happy, easygoing personality. He slept when we slept and got up when we got up. We could bundle him up and take him to a friend's house, where he was content to sit on the floor and play with his toys until he got tired. We could then put a blanket on the couch, and he would go right to sleep.

Scott walked at nine months and also spoke early. He was a happy little boy, but he was lonely. Our living room had a huge bay window. Even as a toddler, he would stand in the window for the longest time, watching the children play in the road out front. "Outside, Mommy," he would say. "Boys, play with boys, Mommy."

Once he was old enough to have playmates, he would get up early, get dressed, and be ready to go to a friend's house.

On October 11, 1962, our second child, Paula Jean Carle, was born, and two-and-a-half-year-old Scott was ecstatic. The day we brought her home from the hospital, he was standing on the balcony of my mother's fourth-floor apartment, waiting for us to arrive. When I got out of the car, he shouted down, "Mom, you got my baby?"

Once I was upstairs, Scott couldn't decide what to do first. He was so happy to see me, but he also wanted to be with his new baby. My mom made lunch, so I put Paula down for a nap. After I had fixed Scott something to eat, I realized he was nowhere to be seen. I went into the bedroom and found him curled up with his pillow and blanket, sound asleep, under her crib.

The next day, as I was dressing the baby, Scott sat on the bed saying "Hello, Paula" over and over again. Suddenly, he laid his head down on the mattress and began to sob. I sat him on my lap and asked what was wrong. His big blue eyes were filled with tears as he said, "She doesn't like me; she won't talk to me."

I hugged him and explained. "New babies can't talk. They have to learn to sit up and get teeth before they can say words."

Five months later, when Paula was sitting up and had a few teeth, we had a replay of that scene. Three-year-old Scott started talking to her and began to cry when she didn't answer. I realized that day that I definitely had to give Scott more information since he had an incredible memory. I then explained that we had to teach her how to talk.

I have the clearest memory of three-year-old Scott kneeling on a kitchen chair in front of Paula's high chair with two objects on the tray. He picked up the first one and said, "Spoon. Say spoon." And then he moved on to the next item, "Ball, say ball." Needless to say, Paula turned out to be a real chatter box.

Scott was a laid-back, easygoing child, and Paula proved to be just the opposite. She was a ball of energy. She hated to go to bed at night and was an early riser. She never walked if she could run, and she adored her big brother. Life with her was never dull. Whenever we were at the park or outside, poor Scott and I were forever chasing after her. Scott had infinite patience with Paula, which was a forerunner of how he would deal with his future sister, Melissa, and brother, Glen.

BIRDS

Scott sat in his navy-blue stroller, kicking his little white high-top shoes and pointing his chubby finger at the sky, shouting "Birds, Mama, birds!" These were two of the first ten words my firstborn toddler had mastered. I didn't realize it at the time, but this was the start of a lifelong love affair.

When he was nine years old, we watched a TV show about chickens. They showed eggs bouncing around as the chicks tried to hatch. Being a city girl, I commented that I hadn't realized how hard it was for a poor little chick to crack an egg.

Scott looked at me and explained, "It's not so hard; that's what they use their egg tooth for."

"Their what?" I asked. I had never heard of an egg tooth.

"It's a tooth on the end of their beak," he said. "They use it to crack the egg, and it falls off after they get out."

"Where did you hear that?" I asked.

"I read it in a bird book."

At precisely that moment, the commentator said, "Of course, this is where their egg tooth comes in handy. It is a small tooth at the end of their beak that helps them crack the shell."

Scott looked over at me and smiled. He didn't say "I told you so" but it certainly was implied.

On every Christmas list, there were bird books of every kind. And he read them all. Whenever we went to the zoo, we always visited the aviary first. Scott would identify each species, what country they were from, and their favorite food. He never had to consult the little plaques; he was a walking bird encyclopedia.

Even as a child, Scott was a wonderful artist. And his most popular subject was birds; he was particularly fond of owls. Soon he was turning out intricate pen-and-ink drawings.

The summer he turned fourteen, he took a drawing class from Evelyn Stebbins, a famous local artist. She encouraged him to enter local art shows to sell his work. He sold enough drawings to afford to purchase an expensive camera. Next, he started taking photographs of birds. He entered a Texas Parks and Wildlife Magazine competition when he was in high school, and one of his bird photos took second place.

The year he turned sixteen, he informed us he was applying for a wild bird license. Without our knowledge, he had sent away to the State of Texas to get the requirements and had worked all year to meet every one of them. It broke my heart to tell him that city ordinances prevented him from having a bird habitat.

Several months later, I came home to find a small gray owl living in a cage he had built when he had planned to buy a cockatoo. It seemed, in his travels around the woods in Nassau Bay, he had found the sick bird. He went out each morning to collect grasshoppers, and other things I didn't want to know about, to feed the baby owl. Unfortunately, the poor owl didn't make it. Scott might have been a six-foot-two football player, but that day he sat down at the kitchen table and cried like a baby.

I hated to drive with Scott. Whenever he got behind the wheel, he would scan the sky for birds. Even as an adult, he would point out birds as he drove. I was always telling him to keep his eyes on the road, but he'd just laugh and say, "But, Mom, it was a red-tailed hawk!"

Even though Scott and his brother, Glen, were almost ten years apart, they were very close. Scott took Glen with him everywhere he went. He began teaching his younger brother about birds at an early age. When Glen was about five, Scott took him to the neighborhood pool. Glen saw a snow-white bird at the water's edge and got really excited.

"Look, Scott, there's a Negro!" he shouted.

Everyone at the pool started to laugh. Scott was mortified. In a loud, clear voice, he said, "It's an egret, an egret."

Years later, before I left for work one day, I decided to take some meat out of the freezer. I found two bubble-wrapped dead birds on one of the shelves. I went upstairs and woke Scott.

"What's with the dead birds in my freezer?" I asked.

"They'll only be there a couple of days, Mom. I'm studying their wing structure and feather patterns."

I told him I was sorry, but they were being evicted that very day.

One afternoon, the police department, where I worked, got a complaint of a suspicious person sneaking around the front yard of a home on Baycrest Drive. The suspect was wearing blue jeans and a red-plaid shirt. The closest unit responded, but the subject was gone.

When I got home from work, Scott was all excited. He began telling me that he had gotten some great photos of baby birds. He had found a dove's nest in the bushes outside a house on Baycrest Drive. I looked at him, and sure enough, he had on blue jeans and a red-plaid shirt.

The next day at work, I marked the call *cleared*. I told the other officers that Scott had been photographing a dove's nest. Most of them had known Scott since he was young. They were accustomed to seeing him in the woods around the city, his camera hanging around his neck in the hopes that he would capture the perfect picture of some exotic bird migrating south for the winter.

They all laughed. "Wish we could have caught him. We would have brought him into the PD in handcuffs. Imagine the look on your face. Maybe we could have charged him with felony birdwatching."

When he was at the University of Houston, he did an amazing self-portrait. Instead of hair, a flock of owls and hawks wove around his head. It really captured the essence of Scott. But for some reason, he drew himself as an old man. I asked why he made himself look so ancient, and he just laughed. Years later, when he was so ill, he said, "It's a good thing I drew that bird portrait, Mom. Now you'll know what I would have looked like if I had gotten old."

Scott had planned to study ornithology, but art finally won out. However, he did have enough credits for a minor in ornithology.

I was surprised when Scott decided to go duck hunting with friends. One year, I asked him how he could shoot a bird when he loved them so much. He patiently explained how many ducks would starve each year due to overpopulation if they weren't hunted.

He began training his black lab, Moe, to fetch ducks. His friend, Jeff, swore Moe would never retrieve a single bird once he was out in the wetlands, so they made a bet. Scott won the bet when Moe performed flawlessly, retrieving every duck. However, Jeff refused to pay up. On the way home, Moe, who was in the bed of the pickup truck, ate all the ducks.

The idea of Scott hunting still seemed strange to me, so I would ask him lots of questions about their trips.

"We line up our pickup trucks at midnight," he described. "Then we walk up and down the line, visiting with friends. I've met guys there I haven't seen since high school. Everyone builds fires, and we talk until the wildlife officers open the site.

"We all walk through the marshes, lugging our decoys. Everyone carries lanterns, and we can hear the alligators hissing at us as we pass by. Then we set up our decoys, lie in the grass, and watch the sun come up. You should hear all the duck calls as they fly in."

He never shot many ducks, and I soon realized it was the camaraderie and the outdoors that he really liked.

Fall now is bittersweet for me. I'll be driving along the road and see the wobbling V formations announcing duck season, and memories of Scott will flood my mind.

A few months after Scott passed away, Melissa got married on our L-shaped backyard deck. The short end of the deck was set up with chairs, and just as Ed and Melissa walked onto the deck, a mourning dove landed on the fence right next to the wedding party. The dove sat there throughout the ceremony. Afterward, Glen said, "Hey, Mom. Did you see Scott? He came to the wedding."

When Ed and I decided to move into downtown Houston, we chose a high-rise apartment in the same building where Glen lives. We were inspecting our new thirteenth-floor unit when a large bird swooped past the living room window. Glen was standing next to me. "Look, Mom. He's one of the red-tailed hawks. They live in that tree over there, and they fly by our apartment building every day. I sit on my balcony and watch them all the time. Wouldn't Scott love this place?"

I held my breath as the hawk soared and dived.

"I've never seen a bird fly at eye level before," I said. "It's awesome and such a unique perspective. Scott would love this view."

We turned, looked at each other, and smiled.

THE ARTIST

As a child, I loved to color and draw, but I lack any artistic talent. As soon as Scott was capable of holding a crayon, I began to purchase art supplies. He enjoyed coloring, but more and more, I saw him gravitate toward plain paper so he could draw.

Right away, his drawings seemed unusual. I showed him how to draw stick figures, but his people were soon potato-shaped with stick arms and legs. Then he began adding eyes and, as his abilities developed, mouths, ears, and noses. Their arms grew large circles at the ends with five small lines radiating outward. One figure had a long, oblong rectangle sticking out behind his neck. When I asked about it, Scott proudly told me, "He's Batman. That's his cape."

Several figures had straight lines at the end of their feet, and I was informed, "They're skiing."

Next, his oval potato people had separate heads. This was long before he entered kindergarten. Finally, I went to the library and checked out a book on children's drawings. I was surprised to read that Scott's drawings were very advanced for his age.

When he started school, his drawing became more complex, and at every parent-teacher conference, the teachers would praise his artwork. I always hung his pictures on the corkboard in the kitchen, and I often chuckled at the stories his work told.

Barbara Ann Carle

Middle school was the first time an elective was offered, and there was no doubt what Scott would choose. With professional instruction, his artwork blossomed. There was always plenty of blank paper at the house, and whenever he had idle time, he would draw. I even began buying sketchpads for him to carry in the car.

In high school, he did intricate pen-and-ink drawings of owls with finely etched feathers. Much of his artwork was featured in school literary publications. The covers of many dramas and musical programs featured his work. The program for a play Scott was singing in featured his line drawing of a flapper in a 1920s hat. After opening night, he came home laughing. "I peeked out from backstage and looked at the audience. All the kids were coloring my drawing with their parents' pens."

Every year, until he went to college, Scott won Houston Rodeo art awards. At one PT conference in high school, his art teacher said, "Your son has the ability to draw a shell that looks like I could pick it up right off the paper, but he is so slow. I keep telling him that when he goes to college and his portfolio is due, the professors won't be willing to wait."

In college, Scott naturally chose art as his major. I don't remember what year it was, but Scott came home one day and announced, "I'm failing art."

"What?" I yelped.

"My portfolio isn't finished, and the professor said if it wasn't ready by today, don't bother turning it in. This represents my final grade."

Later that night, the phone rang, and a man asked to speak to Scott. Scott took the phone into the next room and had a brief conversation. He came back into the kitchen smiling.

"That was my professor. He asked where my portfolio was, and I explained that since it wasn't finished, I didn't turn it in. He then said, 'If I give you another week, would that help?' Of course, I agreed." He smiled. He got an A in that class.

Scott frequently participated in art shows and sold many of his photographs and watercolors. He was also generous with his work. He gave his sisters and brother drawings all the time. I received watercolors for Mother's Day and my birthdays.

Years later, after they were married, Carolyn's friend let them stay at her home in Galveston for a long weekend. Scott sat across the street, drawing the home with the only tools he had available: his sketchpad and a box of children's crayons. Before they left, he propped the sketch up on the kitchen table with a thank-you note. Carolyn's friend and her husband were so excited and pleased with the gift, they had it framed. It still hangs over their fireplace.

Scott continued to sell his work. One day, he researched how to submit the "hidden pictures" featured in the children's Highlight Magazine. These were one- or two-page drawings that had everyday items incorporated into the scene that the children had to seek out and circle. He began submitting his work, receiving one hundred dollars for single pages and two hundred dollars for centerfolds—the two-page ones. Raising four children on a teacher's salary was always a challenge, and these sales supplemented their income. In my closet, I have a stack of these magazines featuring many of his drawings.

Thankfully, Scott's work will live forever in our family and will be handed down through our children to our grandchildren. Whenever I look at his work, I see him—tall, healthy, laboring over his drafting table, smiling as he displayed several new projects—and I have to smile. I'm so grateful to have these precious pieces of his life to see and touch. But in a way, it makes his loss so much worse because I can't help but wonder what he would have created next.

Scott was such a talented man. He carved intricate inlaid mirrors, an amazing tree-shaped wooden jewelry box, and a beautiful wooden sewing box for his wife. He produced wonderful watercolors, oil paintings, charcoal drawings, sketches, and pen-and-ink pictures at will. I can't imagine the body of work he would have amassed, if given the time.

Fortunately, his daughter, Rose, inherited her father's artistic ability. I remember the first time she called and said, "Grandma, my picture won first place in Rodeo Art." She has a wonderful collection of blue ribbons from her early school years, and she went on to win competitions in college, earning prize money that was always helpful.

One day, while we were riding together in the backseat of the car, I realized the many ways she still felt the loss of her father. As she gazed out the window, she wistfully said, "Can you imagine what kind of artist I would be if Dad were here to teach me?"

Her comment brought tears to my eyes. I drew her close. "Your dad is so proud of you, and he's even prouder knowing you've done it on your own."

HEADING SOUTH

Winter was slowly releasing its hold on my backyard. The tree branches were dressed in fat buds just waiting to pop. Pink and white crocuses were beginning to push up through the last thin patches of snow in my garden, a welcome sight on that March afternoon.

I stood at the kitchen sink, washing the lunch dishes. The sound level coming from the family room was acceptable: no shouting or crying. All was well with four-and-a-half-year-old Scott and two-year-old Paula. I was seven months pregnant. My back hurt, my feet were swollen, and I was tired. I remember wishing Ed were home so I could lie down and rest.

I was surprised when I heard the front door open and the kids shouted, "Daddy!" Ed never came home from work early, so I hoped nothing was wrong. He greeted the children and then entered the kitchen.

"Hi, hon, how are you feeling?"

Hating to give the same old answer—*tired*—I smiled.

"I'll put on a pot of coffee, so why don't you sit down. I have a question I want to ask you."

This sounded rather ominous, so I settled down at the kitchen table. Once the coffee was ready, he sat across from me and asked, "How would you like to move to Houston, Texas?"

Barbara Ann Carle

I guess my prolonged silence made him nervous because he began explaining. "You know Grumman was awarded the contract for the Lunar Excursion Module." I nodded. "They've asked me to move to Houston and head up the facilities department. I would be in charge of installing all the equipment needed to test the LEM in the space chamber at the Manned Space Center. I'd also have to set up the off-site office space for all the incoming Grumman personnel. It's a great opportunity."

Ed was thirty-three years old at the time. He had been passed over for a promotion the previous year. They'd said he was more than qualified but was just too young and needed more experience. Now, a year later, they were offering him the chance of a lifetime.

"We wouldn't have to leave until after the baby was born, so don't worry about that." I remember thinking, *Gee, thanks,* but I kept quiet.

"The offer comes with a fifty-percent increase in salary. They'll pay all the moving expenses and set us up in a furnished apartment until we can find a house."

Just two and a half years before, we had built our dream house. It was a four-bedroom tri-level model on three quarters of an acre that was heavily wooded. Our backyard was a veritable forest. The kitchen table sat in a bay-windowed alcove, so as we ate, we were surrounded by white birch, white dogwood, elm, and maple trees. I would have to sell my beautiful home and start all over again.

And then there was my family. My mom, dad, and sister all lived about forty-five minutes away in the city, and I had cousins and friends sprinkled all over Long Island. How could I leave all the people I loved?

Scott wouldn't be starting kindergarten until the fall, which was fortunate. He wouldn't face a big adjustment in that area. But he was so attached to my parents. How would he handle that?

As I sat clutching my coffee cup, I began to get a sinking feeling, but Ed was so excited. "They're going to the moon, Barbara, and we can be a part of it all."

In all honesty, the excitement of putting a man on the moon was

20

contagious. Who wouldn't want to participate in history? I felt my own sense of excitement grow.

Next, he uttered the words that sealed the deal for me. "It's only for two years, three at the most."

How could I stand in his way and disappoint him? After all, I could live anywhere for only two years as long as I knew I'd be coming back home.

I am ashamed to admit, I knew Houston was in Texas but not exactly where. Ed found the atlas, and the distance between New York and Texas looked so very far. Ed kept talking, and his enthusiasm was so contagious that, in spite of my reservations, I agreed.

Of course, deciding to move and actually moving were two different things. Ed made his commitment to Grumman, and we embarked on our major life change. We prepared to put the house on the market and wait for the arrival of the new baby. The company kept their promise, and Ed remained on Long Island for the next four months.

On May 8, 1965, our second daughter, Melissa Louise Carle, was born. She was a beautiful, healthy, easygoing baby, much like Scott. Unlike Paula, Melissa loved to sleep, which was a blessing. Scott was delighted with his new baby sister and immediately began instructing Paula on what was required of a big sister. I found him sitting on the floor one day telling her, "Don't get upset when she doesn't talk to us. She needs to get teeth and learn to sit up. Then we have to teach her how to talk. Don't worry. I'll teach you what to do when the time comes."

Scott wasn't very happy about leaving his grandparents. But we had convinced him we were going on a great adventure, and my parents assured him they would visit soon.

Once Melissa was two months old, the honeymoon was over. Grumman began sending Ed on business trips to California, New Mexico, and Houston. I was left with three young children, trying to keep the house ready to show each time a realtor called.

One afternoon, when Ed was in Houston, the realtor called to say we had two offers on the house. This was long before cell phones, and I had no idea where Ed was working at the Space Center. He always called around six in the evening, so I just had to wait. At six o'clock sharp, the phone rang.

"Hi, hon. One of the guys has invited me to his house for dinner. His wife is waiting downstairs, so I can't talk long. I don't want to keep her waiting."

I guess my patience had reached its limit because I replied, "Oh, okay. I sold the house. Goodbye."

As I was hanging up the phone, I could hear Ed's voice loudly saying, "Barbara, don't you hang up on me."

Well, he calmed me down, came back from Houston, and we sold the house.

Two months later, the papers were all signed. We no longer owned our dream house, and the moving van arrived to pack up all our possessions. It was quite a busy day with me keeping the kids out of the way and Ed making sure the movers loaded everything onto the truck.

By early evening, the moving van finally pulled off down the street. I was giving the living room one last vacuum when, suddenly, all the lights went out. I went outside to see if the whole neighborhood was out of power, only to learn that we were smack dab in the middle of the famous Northeast Blackout. There we were with three small children, no beds, no blankets, no food, and not even a candle.

We sat in the car listening to broadcasts of the statewide ban on driving, which closed all roads and freeways due to lack of traffic lights. We were forced to sneak across Long Island via back roads, trying to avoid police vehicles, so we could reach my cousin Dorothy's house several towns over. Dorothy had five children, and we arrived unannounced on her doorstep with our three little ones. Melissa was the only baby, so the seven older ones ran around playing until we finally got them down for the night. Scott decided moving was a blast.

We were scheduled to be at my mom's house for dinner that night. With no way for us to contact her, she had a pretty sleepless night. We were overjoyed when we arrived at her apartment the next morning. Our plan was to spend two nights there and then head for Houston. My dad was working at a job in New Jersey and wouldn't be home until the following weekend. Late that night, Dad called and said he had been in an automobile accident. He wasn't seriously injured, but he had hurt his back and couldn't work. The next morning, Ed planned to drive my mom to New Jersey and pick him up.

Since we weren't sure how long we would be in our Houston apartment, I had purchased some small Christmas presents for the children. They were hidden under the floor in the back of the station wagon, around the spare tire.

Early the next morning, when Ed and my mom were leaving for New Jersey, they found the trunk of our car open and the spare tire and packages gone. Thankfully, we had carried all our luggage into the apartment the night before. Dollarwise, it wasn't a lot of money, but we now had to put off our trip another two days. The lock had to be repaired, and we needed a new spare tire.

After they left that morning for New Jersey, I sat on the couch and wondered how many more obstacles God was going to put in our path? Maybe we had made a mistake. Maybe we shouldn't be leaving New York.

Three days later, we said goodbye to my sobbing mother and somber father. The reality of leaving my family was much worse than I had expected. We planned to drive to Washington, DC, that day, tour some of the sights, and perhaps spend the night. I think I sniffled most of the way.

Eventually, I pulled myself together. We spent the day showing Scott the Capitol where the laws were passed and the house where the president lived. Of course, Scott was very disappointed when he found out we hadn't been invited to have dinner with the president at the White House. He thought that was the reason we had driven so far.

Early the next morning, we loaded up our kids and pointed the car south.

Finding Home

After driving four days in our new station wagon with a five-year-old, a two-and-a-half-year-old, and our brand-new baby, downtown Houston was a joy to behold. Grumman had rented us a two-bedroom apartment across the freeway from a huge shopping center, Gulf Gate Mall.

As soon as the car was unpacked and we were settled in our new part-time home, Ed headed off to his new exciting job, and I was left in a tiny apartment trying to keep Scott and Paula occupied with a minimum of toys. Every morning, Paula would get out of bed and ask, "I get my tricycle today, Mama?" It was her favorite toy, and she was lost without it. I was left stranded in a strange city without a car, and I didn't know a soul.

One morning, I decided to walk across the overpass to the mall with the children. It was one of those crazy Houston days, where the temperature had dropped twenty degrees, so it was exceptionally cold. I put on my coat, dressed Scott and Paula in winter jackets, and began to dress the baby. The older two started complaining they were hot. We had a first-floor apartment with a large window overlooking the front porch. I sat Scott and Paula on the front step. "Stay right here. I'll be just a few minutes. Don't move."

Just as I finished dressing the baby, I realized I had to change her diaper again. I kept checking outside and the older two sat there looking like little angels. Once outside, I reached down and took Paula's hand. Her hand and the sleeve of her jacket were soaking.

"How did she get wet?" I asked Scott.

"I told her not to put her hand in that pool," he said.

"What pool?"

"The one around the corner. She laid down on the ground and put her hand in the pool. I told her you'd be mad if we didn't come right back, so we ran back."

"Show me."

We turned the corner and between both apartment complexes was a gigantic, unfenced pool. That was the day I learned that Houston had no city ordinance requiring fencing around pools.

I bent down and asked Scott, "What would you have done if Paula had fallen into the pool?"

He looked at me with a big smile and placed both hands on his waist. "I would have jumped in and saved her."

My knees almost buckled. Neither of them could swim, and I realized how close I had come to losing both of them. As long as we lived in that apartment, I never let either one of them out of my sight again.

Our very first weekend in Houston, we began visiting every housing development around the NASA facilities. One afternoon, while Ed and I were driving through Nassau Bay, we passed a beautiful Spanish-style home. We went inside, and it was perfect. Of course, it was on a postage-stamp-sized piece of property. Not exactly what I had expected in the Great State of Texas, but I was in love. At the sales office, we asked about the house. The salesman leaned back in his office chair and shook his head. "You don't want to look at that house. It's much too expensive."

Ed looked at my disappointed face. "Look, just run the numbers, and we'll decide."

He asked Ed about his salary. When Ed answered, the salesman seemed to sit up a little higher in his chair. Next, he asked how much we owed on our car. We had paid cash. And then he asked how much we owed on our credit cards. When I answered, "We owe Sears about a hundred dollars," the salesman shot straight up in his chair.

"You guys can afford that house. Come on, let's go over and take another look."

He had seen a young couple with three small kids and a brand-new car and had decided we must be way in over our heads in debt. We were the ones who almost got away.

Within six weeks, we closed on our new dream house, and the moving van was in the driveway. I ran outside and asked the movers to let me know the minute they found a red tricycle. The second they handed down that bike, Paula was overjoyed. She had her wheels back. Soon, she was peddling away on the concrete patio in the backyard.

All our perishables from the rental apartment—eggs, butter, milk, several sodas, and three cans of beer—were in an ice chest on the kitchen floor. The weather that day was warm and sunny. At one point, in all the confusion, I lost track of Scott. I walked outside and found him sitting on the front step, drinking a can of beer. I was horrified. What a great impression to make on your neighbors when you move into the Bible Belt.

Of course, I didn't have to worry because I didn't have any neighbors. My house was an island surrounded by vacant lots, empty houses, and houses under construction.

I really thought that when we moved into our own house, life would get back to normal. Boy, was I wrong. Ed began working ten- to twelve-hour days, six days a week. Sundays were the exception; he only worked until three o'clock, so we could have dinner together. In addition, he began to travel again. Grumman sent him off to California and New Mexico, and he went back to New York almost every other week. The children missed their dad as much as I did.

The two oldest had no playmates and soon it was time for Scott to go off to kindergarten, leaving Paula totally isolated. Scott was a shy child, and at first, he hated school. He didn't want to leave his sisters and me. But once he realized there were boys and girls to play with at recess, he began to adjust.

Paula was lost without Scott and often sat out on the side steps waiting for him to return. I have to admit, I looked forward to his return just as much. Scott had a wonderful vocabulary, and I could hold almost adult conversations with him. Of course, he did bring home the chicken pox and mumps, which both girls caught. And with Ed gone most of the time, having a house full of sick children was a challenge.

Scott had so much patience with the girls. Kindergarten was full-time in Houston, and he would often come home tired. One afternoon, he looked really beat. He sat at the kitchen table, all sweaty and red faced. Of course, Paula was so excited he was home, she immediately began to pester him to play Candyland, her favorite game.

"No, Paula, I'm too tired."

She just wouldn't stop. "Come on, Scott. Play Candyland. Come on, please."

Scott finally looked at me. "I have two sisters. One I like and one I don't."

Paula's huge blue eyes flew open with surprise. "Mommy, did you hear what he said about the baby?"

I had to cover my mouth. Oh, how typical of my confident little girl. I turned toward Scott and watched him drop his head into the palm of his hand, shaking it back and forth. Defeated, he said, "Okay, Paula, I'll play with you."

I immediately intervened. "No, honey. Scott is going to drink some milk and talk to me for a while. You go play with your dolls and then set up your game. He'll come play in a little while." As usual, she just dashed off into the family room.

"She's so lonely while you're gone. She doesn't mean to be such a pest," I said. "Did anything happen at school?"

"No, we were running races in the playground, and I got so hot."

"It's really hot here, much hotter than back home. But people say we'll get used to it. School is almost out for the summer, and we'll all be going to the pool a lot. Did you know, years ago, they didn't have air conditioning down here? Aren't you glad we moved here after they invented air conditioning?" I smiled.

He smiled back. "Yeah, that would have been awful. I wouldn't have wanted to live here then. I better go play with Paula, Mom. Is Missy sleeping?"

"She'll be up soon."

"Oh, good."

He always enjoyed playing with the girls, which was a great help to me. If ever I was busy, folding laundry or cooking, and one of them acted up, he always tried to amuse them. I never asked for his help; I often told him it wasn't necessary. I had been the oldest child and never wanted to put that responsibility on him. But no matter what I said, he always stepped in to help.

As the vacant houses on our block sold, more and more boys and girls around Scott and Paula's ages moved across the street and down the block. The kids finally had friends and began to adjust to their new environment. We all even adjusted to the heat. Slowly but surely, they forgot about life in New York, and Texas became home.

WINGS

Our life in Houston proved to be totally different from our life in New York. That first year, Ed was immediately sucked into the frantic rush to put a man on the moon. His new job had a very intense schedule.

Ed had always been a hands-on dad, so he made every effort to be home as much as possible. He often came home for lunch, so the girls saw more of him than Scott did. Whenever he could, he'd run home to eat dinner with the family, even if he had to go back to work afterward. And if he couldn't make it to dinner, he'd make sure he was home for the bedtime rituals.

Our free half-days on Sunday became the focus of our week. I always made a huge Sunday dinner, and the rest of the day revolved around the children. Once they were in bed, Ed always filled me in on how the moon-landing project was going: the problems, the successes, and the challenges.

After that first year, things began to normalize a little. Ed worked long hours, but he had most weekends off. He still traveled more than I would have liked, but we managed to have family dinners most evenings.

Ed's habit, when he came home from work, was to pick up the baby, call the other children, and head for the master bedroom. He'd change out of his suit and tie, gather the children on our king-sized bed, and play with them until dinner was ready. This always gave me a welcome break so I could finish preparing our meal. Another nightly habit of his was to go around the house before bedtime, checking to be sure all the doors were locked.

One night, when Ed was out of town, I was preparing dinner when I noticed seven-year-old Scott pick up two-year-old Melissa.

"Come on, Paula," he shouted.

I watched them head for the back of the house, and after a few minutes, I followed. Imagine my surprise when I found the two of them sprawled across our king-sized bed, playing with Melissa. I quietly went back to the kitchen and finished the meal.

When I called out that dinner was ready, they came and sat around the kitchen table just as normal. That night, just before he went to bed, Scott checked the lock on every door in the house. In all the following years that Ed traveled, Scott never varied that routine, and he never checked a lock when his dad was home.

Ed also started the mealtime tradition of "Tell us about your day." Everyone at the table—everyone who could talk, that is—had to tell the rest of the family about their day. We usually started with the youngest, and it was so much fun listening to what they considered to be the highlights or lowlights of their day. This is when we began to realize what a comedian Scott was going to become. His highlights were always exaggerated and his lowlights hysterical.

One day, Scott found a dead bee in the backyard that was in perfect condition, complete with its stinger. While handling it, he pricked his finger with the stinger. Thankfully, the stinger stayed attached. He and I placed the bee on some cotton batting in a small box. Of course, once again, he pricked his finger. Scott intended to take the bee to school for Show and Tell. He even wrote a short paper on bees that he intended to present to his class the next day.

At dinner the next night, Scott told us how his presentation had gone. He had passed the small box around the classroom and asked the students not to touch the bee because of the stinger. His classmates had loved seeing a bee up-close. Next, he had held the bee under a magnifying glass to show them the stinger up-close. He had moved the bee to get a better angle and, sure enough, had gotten stung again. Only this time, the stinger had gone all the way into his finger. The teacher had had to remove it with tweezers. We tried to be sympathetic, but when he started to demonstrate the bee hanging off his finger and him dancing around in pain, we all lost it. His big smile showed me he had achieved the effect he had wanted. We all agreed he belonged in The Guinness Book of World Records as the only boy to be stung three times by a dead bee.

The morning of March 3, 1969, the liftoff of Apollo 9 was due to be televised. Teachers had sent home requests for parents to bring a TV to the school, so the students could watch the telecast. Paula and Scott were all excited. Ed was pretty excited too. This was a big day for Grumman because this was the first test of the Lunar Module in space.

As Scott was leaving for school, he looked really dejected.

"What's up?" I asked.

"No one volunteered. We won't have a TV."

"Oh, I'm so sorry, sweetheart."

"Yeah, I know," he answered, but he looked so down.

When I told Ed, he said, "I'm going to be so busy today."

"I know."

Two minutes later, Ed came from the master bedroom, carrying the spare TV. "I better take off; I don't have much time. I hope I don't have to do a lot of work to get this thing hooked up."

When Scott got home from school that afternoon, he was ecstatic.

"There was this knock on the door, Mom. I looked up, and there was Dad, backing into the room carrying the TV. He looked like a giant. I was so proud that my dad had brought us the TV. The teacher let me stand next to him while he hooked it up. She asked if he could stay and talk to the class, but he said no, he had to get to work. I told them he worked on the Lunar Module. The teacher said to thank Dad and tell him we're going to send him thank-you cards. I was so happy, I could hardly watch the TV. Wasn't it exciting, Mom, watching the liftoff, knowing Dad worked on testing the LEM?"

When Ed got home, I told him he really was Scott's hero that day.

Scott loved nature. He was always reading about birds, animals, or trees. I thought he would really enjoy Boy Scouts. However, when I signed him up for Cub Scouts, I learned a valuable lesson about my son. He was not competitive. He enjoyed the meetings and really enjoyed the desserts, but the rush to get the most badges on his uniform wasn't important. His friend from next door would come by every few days to display his latest badge. Scott would smile, ooh, and aah, and then he would go back to whatever he was doing.

Ed and I were firm believers in children—and not their parents—doing their own work, but we had to poke and prod Scott to get every badge.

One project Scott was interested in was the boxcar derby. Each boy brought home a kit complete with parts, instructions, and rules on the designing and building of a racecar. The parent could offer advice, but the scout was to do all the work alone. Ed gave advice, but Scott sanded, assembled, and painted his car. He was so proud of it.

The night of the race, he placed his car on the start line next to five cars that were obviously built by engineers. In another race, two other boy's cars looked as pathetic as Scott's. Ed took him aside when his car lost.

"Son, I'm really proud of you. You followed all the rules, and that's what counts. This proves it's not just kids that cheat. Sometimes big people cheat too."

When the following year's registration letter arrived, Scott didn't want to rejoin, and we didn't force him.

The Apollo Program ended on December 19, 1972. The Lunar Excursion Module was Grumman's last space contract, and Ed no longer worked in the space industry. However, we were very much a part of the space community. Our friends and neighbors flew on Skylab and the Space Station. Most of our other friends and neighbors worked at NASA, Lockheed, Rockwell, Northrop, or TRW. Our children's friends were all part of that community.

Grumman began winning contracts in the oil industry, so Ed's weekends were free, but the travel continued and, at times, increased.

My children and I have often talked about our life during that time. How would you describe growing up during the height of the space program?

For example, one day my children were playing on our front lawn when a tour bus stopped out front. Tourists began leaning out the windows and taking pictures. My children ran inside and asked me, "Why?"

"It's okay. They're just at the wrong house. They think your dad is an astronaut."

My children rode their bicycles past television vans to visit their friends. They watched the "missing man" formations fly over our home during the funerals of astronauts. They assumed everyone's parents had friends who were astronauts.

We all lived with the successes and the failures of the space program. Did my children admire these men, experience a touch of hero worship? Definitely. They knew these men personally and knew the dangers they faced in outer space. I can't help but feel that this molded their personalities in some ways.

My children watched extraordinary men, who walked in outer space, stand next to Ed in our garage and work on home-improvement projects. They saw extraordinary women, who calmly watched as their husbands were strapped into tiny capsules perched on gigantic, fiery rockets and were launched into space, sit at my kitchen table and discuss cookie recipes. They played with children who said their dads were out of town, a euphemism for walking on the moon.

Kay Cox, my dear friend and fellow writer, once wrote, "We lived extraordinary, ordinary lives." Those words are the closest explanation I can give. How do we articulate a life that was so ordinary to us yet so extraordinary to the rest of the world, but at the same time, was also so extraordinary to us?

My children have all agreed that they loved their lives growing up in Nassau Bay. It was exciting being that close to the people who made history. They are proud that their dad played a part in such a significant moment in time.

The first time I asked if they had been affected by their dad being gone so much, they looked confused.

Finally, Scott laughed. "Mom, everybody's dad was gone all the time. That was just normal. I never even thought about it. Did it bother you guys?"

The other kids shook their heads.

"I just loved going to that little airport on Highway 3 to pick Dad up when he came home," Glen said. "Remember, we got to stand right next to that chain-link fence, near all those small airplanes? You could squeeze your fingers through the holes and almost touch their wings. That was so cool."

They all smiled. Our extraordinary/ordinary lives, once again.

LAST BUT
NOT LEAST

Our two to three years in Houston slowly slipped into four. Ed and I had a decision to make. We both wanted another child, but I was hesitant to face another move with a new baby. But we both agreed it was time. I even suspected I was pregnant with our fourth child, so I scheduled a doctor's appointment.

My fourth pregnancy was more difficult than the other three. On the evening of December 3, 1969, I went into labor. My friend, Bettie, stayed with the children while Ed rushed me to the hospital. After a short, intense labor, our fourth child and second son, Glen John Carle, was born in the early morning hours. However, I suffered some complications during his birth and was bedridden for a week after my three-day stay in the hospital.

The first night at home, Glen woke up at about three in the morning. Ed and I were surprised when the three older kids ran into our room to watch the baby drink his bottle. After we got all four kids back to sleep, Ed looked at me. "I hope this doesn't happen every night."

My first week home was difficult, but on December 14th—just eleven days before Christmas—I was finally allowed out of bed. My mom flew in two days before Christmas, so the holidays that year were very hectic. Even after the children finally went back to school,

Mom stayed for three weeks, so it was late January before life began to settle down.

We had a four-bedroom house in Nassau Bay, so once the baby was sleeping through the night, we had to decide which room he would share. All three children wanted him in their room, but Scott played the gender card. He had so wanted a brother, and he felt the boys should get to share a room.

Scott won that argument.

Scott was nine and a half years older than Glen. I was afraid that they would never be very close due to the age difference, but I could not have been more wrong. Scott was so happy to have a brother, he always spent as much time with Glen as possible. As soon as he got home from school, Scott would immediately begin to play with the baby. And the girls were just as bad. Needless to say, Glen was the star of the family.

Thanks to his three older siblings, Glen spoke very early. By the time he was two years old, he was not only articulate, he was funny. The three older kids were always laughing at what he said.

When Glen was about three years old, he was acting up when Ed tapped him on the butt. Glen looked at Ed. "I don't like you."

Ed answered, "You'll like me a whole lot less after this." And he tapped Glen again.

Glen never changed his expression as he turned to the other kids. "He's right. I do like him a whole lot less."

Of course, the other kids ran out of the room laughing.

The honeymoon of sharing a room with Glen only lasted for Scott until Glen was about three years old. Scott was a very calm child, but Glen was a holy terror. The children all learned to close their doors whenever they left the house—slim protection against the little marauder.

The third time Glen broke one of Scott's model airplanes, the die was cast. Glen had to go, but the question was where? By this time, his two sisters knew their little brother, and neither one wanted him in their room. The girls agreed to share a room; Scott and Glen each got their own.

Scott was a wonderful artist, so he began teaching his brother to draw as soon as he could handle a pencil. Whenever I was busy, if Glen began to act up, Scott would always say, "Come on, Glen. Let's go up to my room and draw." As a result, Glen became a wonderful artist also.

Scott taught Glen archery, photography, and bird-watching. Glen always turned to Scott for advice. Once Scott got his driver's license, he took Glen everywhere he went: The Renaissance festival, Astroworld, Galveston, and the museums in downtown Houston.

I never asked him to take Glen. In fact, I encouraged Scott to go off with his friends on his own. He even once told me his friends would always say, "Don't bring your little brother with you."

"I just laugh and say, 'Don't worry about Glen. He'll be fine.' I take him with me, Mom, because I want to."

I often said it was as if Glen had two fathers.

It amazed me that their friendship continued even when Scott was in college and Glen was in high school. When Scott was at the University of Houston, living in downtown Houston, he would pick Glen up after school on Friday and take him into the city for the weekend. Scott even came home to video-record all Glen's tests for his tae kwon do belts. They talked on the phone almost every day. Glen was best man at Scott's wedding and often visited Scott at work.

When Scott later became ill, Glen was working down the street at Baylor College of Medicine. He ran over to visit Scott every chance he got. He often spent Friday and Saturday nights with Scott. Glen put his whole life on hold so he could be with his brother during that most difficult time.

All my children have felt the loss of their brother, but it was particularly hard on Glen. He seemed lost without his brother. Their relationship had been extra close, and they had shared such varied interests.

Scott was knowledgeable about so many things. His sisters were always calling him for help with art projects, computer problems, and their personal problems. Scott was the perfect sounding board and a great listener. All his siblings turned to him for advice.

His death left a giant hole in the fabric of our family that has never completely mended.

THE MELODY LINGERS

When Scott was in third grade, he came home from school with exciting news.

"Hey, Mom, I've been picked to sing a solo in the school show."

"That's great," I squeaked. I felt my chest and throat muscles begin to constrict. I was horrified. What if he got stage fright, forgot the words, or even worse, was embarrassed. Of course, I was projecting all my personal fears onto my poor son. When God handed out wonderous, melodious vocal cords, He skipped right over me. For me, the thought of singing in front of a packed auditorium was terrifying.

However, Scott was totally unconcerned, and for the next ten days, he walked around the house practicing his solo over and over and over.

The night of the show, I was petrified, all the while trying to look confident and be supportive. In the second act, the curtain rose on a group of six young cowboys gathered around an artificial campfire. The boys with speaking parts said their lines without a hitch. Then my eight-year-old son stood up and faced the audience. His strong voice rang out, every word of "Oh, That Strawberry Roan" loud and clear.

That night, I learned the real meaning of wringing one's hands. By the time he finished, mine were practically bloodless. While everyone applauded, the man in front of us said, "That kid has a really great voice."

I could barely control the urge to grab his shoulder and shout, "That's my son."

Happy it was over, I was just as happy I'd never have to go through that again. Of course, that night was just the beginning. Scott sang in shows, plays, and competitions all through elementary and middle school. And more times than not, it was a solo.

When Scott started high school, he was surprised to find out he had to audition to become a member of choir. After being active since fourth grade, he had assumed he would automatically be accepted into the high school program.

With only one week until tryouts for his solo, he chose as his audition piece "Starry, Starry Night," a popular song about the life of Vincent van Gogh.

"The problem is, I don't know all the words, Mom. While I'm at school, could you listen to the record and write them down for me?"

Ever the helpful mother, I agreed.

For the next two days, I sat on the living room floor, my ear pressed to the hi-fi speaker, playing and replaying that song, copying the words in shorthand, and then transcribing them. Over and over, I heard strains of "Morning fields of amber grain." It is a beautiful, haunting song that describes the tortured life of the artist. Every time I heard the line "Reflect in Vincent's eyes of china blue," I'd think of Scott's eyes. When I was sure I had the lyrics down pat, I handed them over.

Each of the older children had radios in their rooms, so there was always music playing somewhere: popular music with a little bit of country and a little bit of rock-'n'-roll. Thankfully, the three older children's rooms were upstairs. They all had lovely voices and loved to sing, even four-year-old Glen.

Scott and Paula both were in middle school choir. Sometimes, the melody of one of their favorite songs would float through the doorway of one bedroom, and all the kids would come out in the hall, singing along with the radio. It was like I had my own personal choir.

But leading up to tryouts, every radio remained silent. We all listened as Scott walked around the house, or up in his room, practicing "Paint your pallet blue and gray." He had a beautiful, clear, and strong voice, so it was no hardship. However, before it was over, I swear everyone in the house knew that song by heart.

When the big day arrived, Scott was nervous for the first time ever. He so badly wanted to be with his choir friends from middle school. I had no doubt that he would be accepted, so I continued to reassure him. However, I worried all day about how he would feel if the unthinkable happened. When he walked through the back door that afternoon, the big smile on his face told me he had achieved his goal.

Singing was such a big part of Scott's life. Scott sang all the time, around the house, in the shower, in the car, in our motor home, and even while he was painting. It's what made one specific day so painful, when he and I were driving back from MD Anderson. One of his favorite songs came on the radio, and after a few moments, I realized the car was silent.

"How come you're not singing?" I asked.

"Oh, I guess I haven't told you. The radiation has messed with some of my vocal cords. I can't sing anymore. Now don't go getting all upset, Mom. I can still hum."

He laughed. I forced myself to join in.

When I heard those words though, I turned away and struggled to hide the tears that flooded my eyes. Inside, I felt an unbelievable rage at this invisible enemy that had stolen so much from my precious son. A surge of violence I had never experienced before pulsed through my body. I wanted to thrust my hands into Scott's neck, wrap them around that obscene cancer, and rip it free from his body. I wanted to crush it with my bare hands. I experienced a hatred so fierce, I actually shuddered.

"Are you okay, Mom?"

"Yeah, I just got a chill. You know me, I'm always cold. I'll just put my sweater on. Carolyn said I should come back to the house and stay for dinner."

"Oh, good."

"Starry, Starry Night" is a classic and still comes on the radio every so often. When it does, I immediately remember sitting on the floor with my ear up against that speaker. But now its lines evoke different memories.

When I hear "Sketch the trees and the daffodils," I see so many of Scott's beautiful landscapes and florals. Whenever Don McLean sings, "Flaming flowers that brightly blaze, swirling clouds of violet haze," I see Scott leaning over his sketchpad or standing at his easel, working on another watercolor or oil painting.

The line that always brings tears to my eyes is "This world was never meant for one as beautiful as you." It really releases the floodgates.

Those who have never lost a child believe the old adage "Time heals all wounds," but they're wrong. Whenever I hear that song, I am back in my house in Nassau Bay, surrounded by my four laughing children. And when the song ends, all the pain and loss rushes back, as if I had lost him just yesterday. People just don't understand.

"Perhaps they never will . . ."

THE UNIFORM

"Mom, I'm home, and I've got my new football uniform." Nine-year-old Scott backed into the kitchen dragging a four-foot-long mesh bag of football paraphernalia.

My only sibling was a girl, so I was totally unprepared for this event. I stood and stared at the bag. Scott was so excited, he was bouncing up and down. He couldn't wait to open the bag. Of course, Ed was out of town on business, and I was left alone to handle another crisis.

We emptied the bag onto the kitchen table. Game shirt, practice shirt, special socks, a bag of pads that went God only knew where. I gazed at the pile in wonder. I had no idea what to do.

"I think the pads go in the pants, Mom," Scott prompted. The pants had several pockets. One of the pads, a six-inch circle with the top cut off, easily slipped into the pocket at the thigh.

"I don't think that's right, Mom."

Of course, that was obvious since the pocket wasn't round. I am the least mechanically inclined woman I know, and I never scored well at spatial relationships.

The opening for the round pocket at the knee was about four inches wide, much smaller than the pad. I was all thumbs, and I felt like I'd been asked to perform brain surgery. After several attempts, I realized if I folded the pad in half, I could get it into the pocket and then flatten it out. Two down, five to go.

The thigh pad was molded plastic and slid easily into the pocket. I held up the pants. Unless I had seriously misjudged the contour of the human leg, the pad was in backwards. It was hard to mess up the hip pads. They, together with the tailbone pad, snapped into place.

Scott was so excited by then that he was in his underwear and climbing into the pants almost before I got my hands off the snaps.

Next, I tackled the shoulder pads, and of course, once again, I messed up. I fastened them on backward, making it impossible for Scott to move. Both of us were laughing by this time. I was sure I wasn't the only one who wished his Dad was home. He put on his practice shirt and was dancing around the kitchen enthusiastically.

"Now we have to go get cleats," he informed me. "I need them before tomorrow's practice."

Cleats? I didn't even know where to go: A shoe store? A sporting-goods store? Could I get Ed on the phone? I decided to call the coach, who fortunately was a friend of ours.

Next, I helped Scott pull on his helmet and buckle the strap. Well, at least I couldn't get that on backward. I picked up his game shirt and out fell a jock strap. Oh Lord, where was Ed when I needed him? Scott saved the day; he grabbed the package and headed for his room. "I know what to do with this."

See, there really is a God.

The last thing left on the kitchen table was a plastic bag containing the mouthpiece. I took it out of the package and noticed a small, innocent-looking piece of paper float to the floor. I bent over and picked it up.

It read: "Holding the mouthpiece by the strap, which will later be attached to the face guard, immerse in boiling water for forty seconds, then place directly into the mouth. Bite down."

Wait, surely I'd read that wrong. No one would expect a parent to take a plastic mouthpiece out of boiling water and put it directly into their child's mouth. But that's exactly what it said. My God, it would burn his lips, his tongue. What about his gums?

I reached for the phone and was lucky enough to track Ed down.

"Scott got his football uniform today, and I have this mouthpiece thing I'm supposed to boil in water and then put in his mouth. I can't do that. We're talking about boiling water; it will burn his mouth."

"Calm down, Barbara. By the time the plastic reaches his mouth, the temperature will have dropped sufficiently, so it won't burn him."

"I'm not an engineer; I'm his mother. What if you're wrong? Do I just pile all three kids into the station wagon and drive him to the hospital?"

At this point, I realized my son was standing right next to the phone, decked out in his uniform, helmet and all. Through the opening in the helmet, I could see his eyes were as large as saucers.

I had just traumatized him. I was a total failure as a mother, and I was pissed at Ed for putting me in this position. Why was he always out of town when I needed him?

"Okay, Barbara, are you listening? I'll be home by three o'clock tomorrow, plenty of time to do the mouthpiece before practice."

Totally relieved, I hung up the phone and felt the stress drain from my body.

"Dad will be home early tomorrow, so he'll have time to do the mouthpiece," I told my panic-stricken son. The look of pure relief I saw on his face almost brought me to tears.

I piled everyone into the station wagon, headed for the sporting goods store, and got the perfect pair of cleats. At least I got that right.

The next day, Ed made it home on time, as promised. I watched as he placed the mouthpiece into the pot and held my breath as he lifted it out of the boiling water. Thankfully, Scott had retained his faith in his dad, opened his mouth, and bit down. There was no trip to the emergency room, and Scott was overjoyed.

He was proudly decked out in his first football uniform. Ed took him outside and snapped some pictures. In one picture, he stood balancing his helmet on his hip and looked far too old to be my baby boy. I still have that picture.

At four thirty that afternoon, I loaded three very excited nine-year-old boys into my station wagon and dropped them off at practice. The sight that greeted me when I returned was catastrophic. You see, I left out a few things. It had rained all night the night before, and their practice uniforms were white.

I couldn't tell one boy from the other; they were all covered in thick dark-brown gunk. The only reason I knew which one was Scott was because he was the tallest. The only thing still white was their teeth, and I was so delighted to see that Scott's were still intact. I guess that was thanks to the mouthpiece.

We don't have mud in south Texas; we have what we call *gumbo*, a heavy clay-like soil. Their brand-new cleats were packed with that clay and now resembled snowshoes. I loaded the three mudballs into the back of my recently-vacuumed station wagon and watched globs of dirt fall everywhere. I could have wept.

During the drive home, I listened to a conversation between three gleeful nine-year-old boys that no mother needed to hear.

"Did you see Bob Lane? Jimmy Moore hit him so hard, his helmet fell off."

"David Bethel went home with an ice pack on his knee."

"The coach said if you don't fall just right, you can break your leg."

These stories were relayed while they laughed hysterically.

At home, I made Scott strip in the laundry room, and even his underwear was brown. Wrapped in a towel, he headed for the shower while I tackled his uniform and wire-brushed his cleats.

That day, I started a relationship with those clothes that lasted through four years of Little League football. Two or three times a week, depending on the weather, I disassembled, washed, bleached, dried, and reassembled that uniform. Fortunately, in junior high and high school, the school staff took over that job.

One Thanksgiving, years later when Scott was a grown man, he called down the length of the dining room table. "Hey, Mom, remember the day I brought my football uniform home?"

I froze and nodded. I had so hoped he had forgotten that day. He got a twinkle in his eye that I'd seen so many times before. "Remember the mouthpiece?" His booming laughter filled the room, and I lost it. Ed, Scott, and I shared a good, long laugh.

The other three children looked puzzled. I suddenly realized that Scott and I had been alone that day. The girls had been off playing at their friend Alayne's house, and I had been pregnant with Glen at the time. Scott had been the sole witness to my motherly meltdown, but that private moment didn't stay private for long. There was nothing the other kids enjoyed more than a family story that embarrassed Mom.

So Scott regaled them with the tale of the uniform fiasco. Of course, he embellished the whole story and made me sound far more incompetent than I remembered. His demonstration of how he had had to walk after I put the pads in the pants backwards, stumbling around the dining room with his knees and toes touching, was a gross exaggeration. And the part about the steam coming out of my ears and nose was pure fabrication.

However, it was so funny, and soon the entire family was holding their sides, rolling in their chairs. And the warmth and love I saw in Scott's eyes and heard in his voice softened the tale of my battle with his football uniform.

So I guess the moral of the story is that sometimes you think you've failed your children, and sometimes they love you anyway.

THE SUPERHERO

"Mom, I think I have a problem. Glen and Bob came up to my room today and told me they think it's time I started fighting crime."

Scott became interested in archery when he was sixteen. He began purchasing bows and other equipment on our trips to the flea market in Canton, Texas. The day Scott set up a practice target in the backyard, Glen decided that whatever Scott could do, he could do too. And when Glen wanted to do something, he could be quite persistent.

Pretty soon all we heard was, "Can I try? Can I try?"

Scott began searching for a bow that Glen could handle. When he found the right size, he began giving archery lessons to Glen and Glen's best friend, Bob.

When it came to Glen, Scott had infinite patience, so eventually they were out back every evening, practicing. After about a year, both boys were quite proficient.

That fall, Scott took Glen to the Renaissance festival. He said three men in their twenties had been playing the archery game, and they had been really awful. It had been obvious they didn't know the first thing about archery. Glen had decided he wanted to try. The three men had begun to laugh at the seven-year-old kid who wanted to try to shoot an arrow. With a fair amount of pride, Scott laughed when he described the scene.

"I stood off to one side. Glen walked up to the stand, put down his money, and took the proper stance. He pulled back the string in perfect form and scored three out of three shots. Those older guys were stunned."

And that's what led to Scott's dilemma.

"Now Glen and Bob want me to become a superhero. They think I should buy green tights and a green shirt and go out at night with my bow and arrows to catch bad guys. I tried telling them I couldn't do that, but they're convinced I can. I don't know what to do." Scott was eighteen at the time, and Glen was almost eight.

Scott and I had a good laugh. The thought of him running around Nassau Bay in green tights with a bow and a quiver of arrows on his back was just too funny.

"You have to admit, it's rather flattering that they're convinced you can be a crime-fighter." I couldn't help adding, "And come to think of it, you do look rather good in green."

Poor Scott was between the proverbial rock and a hard place. Glen idolized his big brother and thought he could do anything.

"I don't want to hurt their feelings, but they just won't take no for an answer," Scott said.

"Don't worry," I said. "I'll talk to Glen."

The next day, when Glen came home from school, I sat him down. "So Scott told me you have a plan for him. You and Bob want him to go out at night and become a crime-fighter."

The enthusiasm that lit his face showed me just what I was up against.

"Yeah, Scott's a great archer, Mom. He'd be really good at going out after dark and looking for bad guys."

"Well, honey, you know he can't go around arresting people; he's not a police officer. The police department wouldn't want him doing that."

"There are bad guys out there, right? You're a police officer, Mom, and you go after bad guys all the time."

"Well, yes, but that's my job, and it's what I've been trained to do. Police officers don't want citizens running around trying to catch criminals. It's too dangerous. That's what we're paid to do."

"So we won't tell them. You, Bob, and I can keep it a secret."

"But what if Scott gets hurt?"

"Oh, he won't get hurt; he's too good. You should see him, Mom, he never misses."

"I know he's good, but what if the bad guy has a gun?" I asked.

"Oh, he's really fast, Mom. He wouldn't get hurt. So will you make his outfit, Mom? He needs green tights and a green shirt. Maybe a hat too. He could look like the Green Arrow."

I was getting nowhere fast. I knew Scott was an excellent archer, but I doubted he was faster than a speeding bullet.

"You know Scott is really busy. He goes to school, and he works. He has lots of things he needs to do."

"That's why Bob and I will help. Will you make us outfits too, just like Scott's? And then when Scott's busy, Bob and I can take over."

"I don't think Bob's mom would let him become a crime-fighter," I replied.

"She will if you talk to her. I know you can convince her."

I found myself face to face with a major case of hero worship. How could I maintain the image Glen had of his brother and, at the same time, talk some sense into him?

"You know Scott starts college in two months, right?"

"Yeah."

"And you know college is really hard, right?"

He nodded his head.

"Well, he couldn't possibly attend classes, do his homework, study, and work while being a crime fighter, could he? And you know how much he's looking forward to going to college. We wouldn't want him to fail, would we?"

I could see his blue eyes cloud with a look of deep disappointment. I got a dejected "No."

Shoulders slumped, he turned and walked away. At the last

minute, just before going through the doorway, he spun around, smiling, and shouted

"That's okay, Mom. He can do it on his summer vacation."

THE ANNIVERSARY

I had never dreamed that September 6, 1984, would come so fast. But that day, Ed and I had been married for twenty-five years. We reviewed those years the night before. Ed and I agreed our life had turned out pretty amazing. The one goal we had to put off was our planned anniversary trip to Hawaii. With three kids in college, it just wasn't feasible. We decided that doing it for our thirtieth anniversary sounded just as good. It seemed like a small sacrifice to pay for the great life we were leading.

The children planned a small dinner party for the family and asked if we would come home early. I arrived at the house around three thirty in the afternoon. I had made a pot of my famous spaghetti sauce the day before, so all I had to do was prepare the pasta. The girls had baked a delicious-looking chocolate cake. We were all disappointed when the phone rang, and Ed announced he was stuck at work but would be home as soon as possible.

Scott was twenty-four years old and studying at the University of Houston for his master of art education. Paula was almost twenty-two and was a senior at the University of Houston / Clear Lake, studying for her bachelor's degree in accounting, while Melissa was nineteen and a sophomore attending San Jacinto College. Glen was fourteen and the only one not in college. He was a freshman at Clear Creek High School.

I knew Scott had a night class, and Melissa was scheduled to work at the mall that night. The three oldest kept pacing around the family room. I felt they were worried Ed might be extra late.

While we were waiting for Ed, Glen handed me a medium-sized box. "Hey, Mom, do you want to open your present from me now, or do you want to wait until Dad gets home?"

Of course, I answered, "No, let's wait for Dad." Glen was a wonderful artist, thanks to Scott's tutoring, so I figured he had drawn us a picture.

The whole family cheered when the back door opened at 4:45 p.m. and Ed walked in.

Before we could sit down for dinner, the kids announced they had a present for us and wanted to give it to us immediately. They handed us a large, beautifully wrapped package. In the box was an eleven-by-thirteen-inch framed photograph of the four children, something Ed and I had wanted for a long time. I was overjoyed and passed the picture to Ed. Scott had taken a timed photo at Armand Bayou Park in Clear Lake City. Of course, then the whole story of how the picture was taken came out.

"We picked a day the girls could get home early," Scott said, "and I talked to Glen's teachers and took him out of school for the afternoon. We came home so he could put on his suit and tie, but when we arrived, your car was in the driveway. Since I was due home from school anyway, I put Glen in the motor home and came inside. That was the day you came home from work with the flu, remember?"

Since my bedroom was right next to the staircase, they couldn't sneak upstairs without me knowing. The motor home was stored under the carport, which was right under Scott's bedroom window. So when the girls got home, they and Glen climbed on top of the motor home and climbed in through Scott's window.

"We had to tiptoe around in our bedrooms as we got our clothes." Paula laughed. "It was really hard for me since my room is right over yours."

"And we all know how quiet Paula is," Glen teased.

"We did our makeup and fixed our hair as quietly as possible," Melissa said. "Since you knew Scott was home, he went outside. We passed our clothes down to him, climbed out the window, and we all got dressed in the motor home. You slept through the whole thing."

"But it took us so long, Scott didn't have time to shave. He grabbed his razor and shaving cream. He was going to shave in the restroom at the park, but when we got there, it was locked." Glen laughed.

"See the little pond on the left side of the picture?" Scott asked. "That's where I shaved."

Scott showed me the proof sheet, and it held my favorite picture of our children. The timer had gone off before they were ready. The four of them, dressed in their Sunday best, were standing everywhere in the frame. Melissa was bent over at the waist, Paula was facing the camera, Scott's head was thrown back, and Glen was clutching his stomach. It was obvious they were laughing so hard they could hardly talk. It's the way I'll always remember them.

Next, Glen handed me the small, slim box I assumed was his present. I opened it, and nestled in the white tissue paper was an itinerary from the local travel agency. It included plane tickets and hotel reservations for an eight-day, two-island trip to Hawaii scheduled for three weeks from that night. I was stunned and began to cry.

"It's just a picture of the kids," Ed said. "What the heck are you crying about?"

I handed him the box, and he immediately said, "We can't accept this; it's way too much."

The kids all laughed, and Scott said, "You better accept it. It's all paid for." Of course, then the other story came out.

"A year ago, right after your last anniversary," Paula said, "Scott called a family meeting. He had gone to the travel agency and gotten all the information. 'If we start saving now,' he said, 'we could send Mom and Dad to Hawaii on their twenty-fifth wedding anniversary.'"

The three oldest were all in college and working twenty hours a week at part-time jobs. Scott worked at a frame shop in downtown

Houston, Paula worked in the accounting department at Grumman, and Melissa worked at Morrow's Nut and Candy Shop at the local mall.

"We divided the amount we needed to raise into four equal shares and started saving our money," Melissa said.

"You'll never have as much fun in Hawaii as we had lying up on my bed, counting our money," Paula added.

Her words reminded me of how much time the four of them had spent upstairs over the past year. I had assumed they were getting along so well because they were older.

"The room rates are according to location," Glen said. "The cheapest rooms face the parking lot. First, we saved enough for the parking lot, and Scott said, 'Let's shoot for the pool.' We eventually had enough to afford the mountain-view, but we never did save enough to face the ocean, Mom."

I pulled him close. "Don't worry, sweetheart. This is perfect."

"I went to visit each of your bosses," Scott said. "They thought it was great. They both agreed to give you guys the time off. Everything is all arranged."

It turned out everyone at both our work places knew about the surprise. All through our quick dinner and dessert, the main topic was the trip and how they had managed to keep it secret.

Before Scott left for his class, he pulled me aside. "The girls and I had a separate meeting. We knew Glen could never raise his full share. We agreed to make up the difference. I wanted you to know that the little stinker almost paid his whole part. He pitched in his weekly allowance, his birthday money, and his Christmas money. The girls and I only had to add a little bit."

I laughed as I remembered how many times Glen had asked for extra money and had had to endure my "That's what your allowance is for" sermon. Then there were all the excuses he'd come up with for not having any money.

I also recalled Scott being disappointed when he didn't win first place in an art show. I had used the fact that we weren't going to Hawaii as an example of life's little disappointments

"How did you keep a straight face?" I asked him. He beamed.

Now, don't get the impression that my children were angels. They weren't. They had their fair share of quarrels and fights. But that night, as far as Ed and I were concerned, they were perfect.

Scott was the ringleader in our family, and it amazed me how enthusiastically the others always followed his lead. He would organize surprise birthday parties for his siblings and think of special gifts for Ed or me. But this was a huge undertaking and way beyond anything Ed and I had ever expected.

Well, Ed and I went to Hawaii, and we had a blast. We took tons of pictures, and one night after we returned, we all gathered in the family room for a slide show. We gave each child a special gift: The girls got coral and diamond rings. Scott received two beautiful original watercolors of native Hawaiians and a lovely ocean landscape. Glen got a carved-bone-handled Samurai knife.

However, we knew we could never repay the gift they had given us.

THE GROOM

B end down and stand still. I'd rather not shed any blood while I pin on your boutonniere."

Scott chuckled. "Hey Glen, maybe you better get Mom the ladder."

Nothing brought more joy to my children than the fact that they were all taller than their mother. I remember the first time I turned to hand something to Scott and found we were no longer eye to eye. Mothers always expect to be larger than their children, so the day they're not, it is a shock.

I was pretty adept at boutonnieres. I had attached several to Scott's lapels for proms and his friends' weddings. But that day he couldn't stand still. That day was different. That day, he was getting married.

Scott had dated Carolyn Chandler in high school, but they had gone their separate ways after graduation. She headed off to the University of Texas, and he attended the University of Houston. Years later, they ran into each other downtown and began dating again. Scott had just graduated with his master's degree in May, and he was working at his first teaching job.

That June day, Ed and I were not only getting a new daughter-in-law but were also getting three instant grandchildren. Joshua would be four on July 3rd, and the twins, Emily and Sarah, would be three on July 17th. We were delighted. Some people questioned whether Scott should take on the responsibility of three children, but I knew Scott. He loved children.

When his three youngest siblings were babies, they reached for Scott as quickly as Ed or me. Their first three words were Mama, Dada, and "Sott." He was amazing with the youngest ones, and he always made time to play with them. In church, Scott always pointed out cute babies.

When Glen was a toddler, we decided to put him in the church nursery. He began to cry, so Scott offered to stay with him. Glen hung onto Scott for a good while, but eventually he began playing with another boy. With Glen amused, Scott offered to assist with the other toddlers. When we picked up the boys, the mothers there were so impressed with Scott and how wonderful he was with the children.

The next week, Glen wanted Scott to stay again, and he agreed. Scott enjoyed working in the nursery so much that he agreed to stay on as a volunteer for the next three years. When Scott could no longer volunteer, the mothers at the nursery were so sorry to see him leave. They said he had been invaluable to them.

When Scott was about fourteen, he came home from school one day and found me lying on the couch. I got up. "I've got something to tell you."

"You're pregnant," he said.

"No, why would you say that?"

"Well, when you were pregnant with Glen, you were lying on the couch a lot when we got home from school."

"No. I just wanted to tell you my grandmother is coming to visit us. Would you want me to have another baby?"

"Well, Glen will be five years old soon. It would be nice to have another baby around the house again."

I always knew Scott loved children, but that day was proof positive.

The wedding took place in the backyard garden of Carolyn's parents'. The day before, we had practiced the ceremony, carefully demonstrating the procedure. Emily and Sarah would walk in front of the bride, carrying baskets of rose petals. Since Sarah is deaf and was only three years old at the time, we had pantomimed throwing petals out of empty baskets to show the girls exactly what to do.

The day of the wedding was a scorcher, even by Houston's standards. We were a small group, just family and friends. As we stood in the backyard, our guests from New York seemed to gradually melt before my eyes. I finally moved them out of the sun and under a small group of trees.

Joshua stood next to Scott, looking adorable in his little tuxedo. The backdoor opened, and Emily walked out dressed in a beautiful pink satin dress, her golden hair crowned in a ring of pink flowers. She carefully tossed the rose petals onto the grass.

Sarah followed in a matching dress and hair piece. It immediately became obvious that we had failed to explain what was expected of her. When she saw all the rose petals littering her grandmother's beautiful backyard, she covered her mouth with her hand and began scooping them up, putting them in her basket.

Those of us who could, frantically signed, "No, it's okay." The bride had to rush out, crouch down, and explain that *yes*, they were supposed to toss the rose petals onto the ground. Poor Emily just stood there, her hands on her hips, almost in tears. She had done exactly as she was told. She didn't understand why everyone was laughing. Carolyn took both girls back inside and calmed everyone down, and we started over.

The door opened and out walked Emily looking very put upon. She began throwing her rose petals and broke into a huge smile when we began to applaud. Following came Sarah looking slightly confused. She shrugged her shoulders and began throwing her rose petals, perhaps a little too enthusiastically. We all chuckled, but she smiled when she realized we were applauding.

The bride looked radiant in a white satin-and-lace mid-calf dress. She carried a bouquet of red roses. Second time was the charm, and the wedding went off without a hitch.

As soon as the wedding was over, we all headed to the Watergate Marina, where the reception was being held. All their guests were waiting at the Kevin's Cove restaurant. Carolyn's parents had reserved a large private room on the second floor, where the food, wedding cake, and bar were located. A large wooden deck, right outside, had several tables that overlooked the marina, with Galveston Bay in the background. A stairway led down to a huge brick patio with additional tables around the dance floor and the stage.

Scott's favorite musician was Shake Russell. From the time they were in high school, Scott and his friends had been following him all around Texas. At one point, he and his band had gone to Nashville and recorded some national hits. But like Willie Nelson, they had come back home to Texas. As a wedding gift, Carolyn had arranged for Shake Russell and his band to play at the wedding. Scott and his friends were all so surprised.

Ed and I settled all our family members visiting from New York at two tables on the upper deck. This afforded them a perfect view as the sun set behind the marina. It was also accessible to the cool breezes that rolled in off the water. All the young people grabbed tables on the patio, close to the band. Soon after we arrived, the speeches were made, the food was served, the cake was cut, and most important, the champagne began to flow.

Throughout the late afternoon and early evening, I watched Scott dance with his new bride, laugh and talk with his brother, sisters, and friends, and sit with Joshua, deep in conversation as they laughed and laughed. Later, he danced with little Emily, her tiny feet standing on top of his black dress shoes. He would lean down to talk to her, and she would giggle. Scott took Sarah up to the band and held her hand up-close, so she could feel the vibrations of the music. Both her hands in his, they swayed back and forth, with Scott occasionally signing a few words. She stared intently up at him, smiling, so proud to be dancing just like everyone else.

Scott and Carolyn looked so happy. I remember thinking he had finally found the life he had always been looking for.

As the sun set, the welcomed breezes began to pick up. I was standing upstairs, leaning on the railing and watching the crowd below move around the dance floor, when suddenly Scott was standing beside me.

"It was a nice reception, wasn't it, Mom."

"Everything was wonderful, Scott: the food, the cake, especially the music."

"Did you have a good time?"

"I had a great time. I even got Dad to dance more than one dance with me."

He smiled and handed me an ice-cold unopened bottle of champagne.

"I thought you and Dad might like to take this home with you. Maybe have a few drinks later."

I laughed. "What a good idea."

"Shake wrote a really nice message to Carolyn and me on the back of one of his albums. Wasn't that nice of him?"

"That really was."

He laughed. "I guess I better get back downstairs." He leaned over and kissed my cheek. "I love you, Mom."

"I love you too, sweetheart."

He laughed again and ran back down the stairs.

As the crowd began to thin, Shake played his most famous hits, and everyone joined in for a sing-along.

We bid goodbye to all our guests, and the family headed back to our house.

The day had ended, and Scott was a married man.

FATHERHOOD

Scott really embraced fatherhood. He and Carolyn had rented a house in Clear Lake City, which wouldn't be ready for a month. Scott asked if they could stay with us until then. We had plenty of room, so of course we agreed. For Ed and me, it was such a pleasure having a house full of little people again.

As I watched Scott with his new family, I realized he hadn't lost any of the patience or talents he had displayed with his siblings. He still had that laid-back attitude around the kids and could always make them laugh.

Since Carolyn was working and Scott was off for the summer, they decided to keep the children out of day care. One of the first outings he planned was to take all three of them to the Houston Children's Museum, a huge undertaking even in my eyes.

After waiting in line for close to an hour and with the box office in sight, he noticed that the twins were wiggling around. When he asked what was wrong, Sarah signed, "Restroom," while Emily said, "We have to pee." He quickly headed for the nearest bathroom. When they returned, the line was twice as long as before. But Scott wasn't just the oldest of four siblings. Over the years, he had become my right-hand man. He knew exactly what to do.

"Do you guys want to go get ice cream and come back another day when it's not so crowded?" he asked.

One sign and two shouts of "Yes!" and they were off. He returned home hot and tired, but with three happy campers.

The first thing Scott and Carolyn did after the wedding was hire a sign language teacher to come to our house. Once a week, every member of our family gathered together so she could teach us how to communicate with Sarah. It is difficult to learn a new language, but the whole family worked really hard to master at least rudimentary signing.

After they moved out, Scott rarely came to visit without the three kids. I'd often run into Scott in stores throughout Nassau Bay, and he was never alone. He always had his three children in tow.

Scott was a hands-on dad. He attended every play, sports activity, and teacher's conference. One year, Scott and Glen coached the twins' softball teams. When they won second place in their league, the woman who delivered the news told Scott, "This was such a pleasure for me. I got to tell each coach that your girls came in second. 'Mr. Carle and his brother never once yelled at their girls. They never got angry or lost their tempers. They thought the girls should have fun, and none of their girls ever cried.'"

Scott and Glen couldn't understand why someone would make seven-year-old girls cry over softball.

Scott and Carolyn eventually moved to Nassau Bay and once the girls joined the swim team, Scott was out there volunteering every weekend. He helped the team purchase an electric start gun that flashed a light, since Sarah could not hear the traditional one.

Scott and Carolyn became very active in the deaf community. Scott arranged for me, in my police uniform, to come to the deaf unit at Clear Creek School District and sign a bicycle safety class. With him as my interpreter, I even answered questions afterward: from the standard "had I ever shot someone?"—"No"—to "was a woman police officer allowed to wear nail polish on duty?"—"Yes." Scott was also the signing Santa Claus for all the classes and parties at Christmas time.

Scott, decked out in a suit and tie, attended the Girl Scouts

Father/Daughter dances with Sarah and Emily. Carolyn, who is an amazing seamstress, made beautiful red-plaid taffeta and black velvet dresses for the twins. They made quite a trio.

Scott was just as involved with Joshua. He taught him how to use a computer and encouraged Josh, who is so intelligent, to read up on programming and try it. Scott attended all his baseball games and was often out in the backyard with Joshua practicing his batting and catching skills.

Joshua was an avid reader from a very young age and found a true friend in Scott. Their shared love of reading led to swapping books, and Scott got to recommend all his old-time favorites: *The Hobbit*, *Dune*, and *The Lord of the Rings*.

Scott even got to take the whole family fishing and taught them how to bait their hooks. He would make up and sing little jingles, imitate the voices of cartoon characters, and make up amazing stories that kept the kids mesmerized. I've heard people talk about finding their inner child. Scott never lost his inner child. It was always lurking under the surface, ready to jump out and come play, whether with children or adults. That's why he could always make us laugh.

I'm not saying there weren't conflicts. Lord knows, you can't raise a houseful of children without conflict. And Scott always worried if it was because he was their step-father. But I reasoned that if that was the case, since he was raised with his real mom and dad, we should have lived in perfect peace and harmony. We both got a good laugh out of that.

Our back door opened one afternoon, and the whole gang piled into the family room. Scott said, "Sarah has something she wants to tell you."

Sarah was eight years old, excited, and giggling.

"Go ahead, tell them," Scott signed.

She smiled, touched Carolyn's stomach, and signed, "Momma has a baby in there."

That's how Ed and I learned we were about to become biological grandparents for the first time.

"Just think, Mom. Carolyn had one set of twins. If she has another, I could end up with five children, one more than you and Dad." Scott thought that was hilarious.

On July 23, 1991—Scott's birthday—his first child, Rose Beth Carle, was born. He was so happy, proud, and excited. However, Rose was born early, and the doctor soon broke the news: her lungs were not fully developed. She needed to be transferred by ambulance to St. Joseph's prenatal hospital in downtown Houston. The hospital sent a doctor, a full staff of nurses, and not one but two ambulances, each equipped with an incubator. The doctor explained that they didn't want to take the chance that one ambulance might break down.

I stayed with Carolyn, while Ed and Scott followed the emergency vehicles. As they sped through the night, Scott looked at Ed. "I think I just met my deductible."

The day Rose was released from the hospital, Scott stopped by the police department to show off his beautiful little girl. As he was leaving, he said, "The day she was born went from the best day of my life to the worst. I was so afraid we were going to lose her. But today she was released with a clean bill of health, and I couldn't be happier."

Scott loved the three older children, but Rose was his family's first baby, and oh, how he loved babies! He bathed her, dressed her, changed her diapers, and even took her to work. And with all his experience, he was an expert on teaching babies to talk. He even enlisted Emily and Joshua's help, so Rose spoke really early.

The people he worked with couldn't believe her vocabulary. One teacher had a little one the same age as Rose, so one day when Scott was up at school, he said, "Rose, tell Mrs. Winters where we just were."

Rose answered, "The pharmacy."

The woman almost fell out of her chair. "My little guy just about says 'Mama' and she can say 'pharmacy'?"

Scott was always so proud.

Whenever he entered our back door those days, he had four children with him, with Rose riding on his hip. One day, when Rose was about a year and a half, Scott came over and stood Rose on our kitchen countertop.

"Rose," he said. "Sing the Pops opera."

She spread her two little arms and sang loudly, "POPSSS. POPSSS."

It was so funny. We couldn't stop laughing.

For two years, his life seemed so perfect. The older children began to spend more time with their friends. Sarah left home for the Texas School for the Deaf in Austin. She was a student there from middle school through high school. It was sad for our family; we all missed her so much. But it was so beneficial for her. The educational opportunities were greater, and her social life improved.

Scott enjoyed every minute he spent with his expanded family, but his diagnosis changed so many things. The older children understood the seriousness of his illness, but how much did his precious two-and-a-half-year-old understand? They both suffered when he was in the hospital. She didn't understand why Daddy had to go away so often. She just wanted her daddy home.

When Scott was having radiation treatment, she wanted him to draw purple lines on her neck, just like his. She wanted Carolyn to take a picture so everyone could see that she looked just like her daddy.

After one of his more radical surgeries, Scott and I were dropping her off at a church preschool program. He was about to walk her in when she said, "Maybe Grandma could walk me in. Some of the kids might be afraid of your hospital neck."

"Oh, are you afraid of my hospital neck, honey?"

"Oh no, Dad. I like your hospital neck. I just don't like the hospital."

Scott just laughed. "Okay, Grandma will walk you in."

When I returned, he looked at me. "What am I going to do? She's so damn smart. I've got to get better, Mom. I love her so much; I can't leave her."

All during his illness, he tried to give the children a normal childhood. He was so into Christmas and, even toward the end, tried to act as normal as possible. The older children knew his condition was worsening. But we never knew how much Rose understood. As sick as he was, Scott would still play Barbie dolls with her and read to her. He wanted to be a real dad to her for as long as he could.

Once a month, Scott was hospitalized for intense treatments. Ed would return to Florida following his release and I would remain in Houston as long as needed. He was often very ill while he recuperated at home. Every morning, I'd try to arrive at his house before he and Rose were awake. Carolyn would have left for work, and the older children were at school.

One day, I got stuck in traffic and was later than usual. Four-year-old Rose met me at the door, delighted that I had brought donuts. I walked into the master bedroom and found Scott with his arm across his eyes, obviously in tears.

"When she woke up and you weren't here, she said, 'Grandma isn't here, Daddy. Who's going to take care of us?' My own daughter doesn't think I can take care of her. I have got to get out of bed today and sit on the couch. I can't have her remember me as someone who couldn't even take care of her."

I cursed the traffic that had delayed me and quickly helped Scott out onto the couch. I watched him play with Rose, making her giggle, hugging and kissing her, and once more I asked God, "Why?"

FACING FACTS

The morning after Scott told us he had cancer, I awoke early and began to fight off a feeling of dread. Scott had so much going for him. He was young and healthy. The cancer had been contained within the boundaries of the biopsy. We were fortunate enough to live less than thirty miles from one of the largest, most famous cancer hospitals in the nation. I vowed to remain confident.

The next week, Scott, Carolyn, Ed, and I wove through the halls of MD Anderson Cancer Center in downtown Houston. We met with a doctor who reviewed Scott's medical records and outlined his plan for Scott's treatment. He would have surgery at the end of May and, after the incision had healed, two months of radiation. The doctor was very positive; he was happy to have a patient in great physical condition with no other medical problems. The surgeon finished our visit by shaking Scott's hand and saying, "See you in surgery."

Ed had worked for Northrop Grumman for close to forty years by then. Several months prior to Scott's diagnosis, the company had closed their Houston facility. They had asked Ed to relocate to St. Augustine, Florida, for a few years. After talking it over with the family, Ed had accepted the short-term assignment.

Since our stay in Florida would be temporary, we hadn't sold the house. Glen had just graduated from the University of Houston and would be living at home with Melissa and her husband, A.J. Ed was scheduled to report to St. Augustine just days after Scott had shared the results of his biopsy. Ed notified the company, and his departure was put off, pending the outcome of Scott's surgery.

At the end of May, Scott entered the hospital and had his surgery. They removed a much larger area of flesh than we had expected but Scott recovered quickly. The surgical biopsy came back, and the doctor was very pleased with the results. Scott would need two months of radiation. Since he worked in education and school was closed for the summer, he was free to go back and forth for his treatments without missing any work.

The surgery had gone so well, we decided Ed could head for Florida and I would stay in Houston while Scott completed his radiation. He tolerated the treatment very well, only getting tired toward the end.

Scott's treatment was completed by the end of August, and all his tests came back negative. The doctor was delighted and gave him an eighty-percent chance that the cancer would not reoccur. We were all extremely optimistic.

I moved to St. Augustine with plans that we would be home for Christmas. I kept in touch with Scott, the other children, and my mother by phone. Everyone assured me that Scott was doing great. He was happy and was even gaining weight, but I hated being so far away. Fortunately, Melissa worked for Southwest Airlines, so Ed and I had free flight benefits. We could return to Houston immediately if we were needed.

As the holidays approached, I was anxious to get home. Ed was involved with a project, so we weren't free until Christmas. This was the first Thanksgiving all the family wasn't together. Paula and her husband, Mark, decided to come to Florida for Thanksgiving, so that helped. My mother came the second week in December and flew back to Houston with Ed and me just days before Christmas.

The entire family was at the house when we arrived. Everything looked beautiful. All the decorations were up, including the Christmas tree. Everyone was so glad that we were home.

Scott asked me to come upstairs to see some of his latest drawings. Once we were alone, he said, "Mom, I have something to tell you. There's a lump on my neck. It showed up a few days before I was scheduled for my three-month checkup. It was biopsied last week, and I'm waiting for the results."

I was stunned. When I had walked into the house, I had noticed that Scott looked so much better physically, heavier and stronger. But after a big hug and kiss, he had had trouble looking me in the eye. Now I knew why. A few hours later, the call came. It was malignant. We were scheduled to see a new set of doctors at MD Anderson two days after Christmas.

Scott was determined to enjoy the holidays. This was the first time Rose really understood Christmas. She was three and a half years old and so excited. Santa Claus was coming to her house. On Christmas Eve, I wished Scott and Carolyn good luck on getting her to sleep.

At eight o'clock on Christmas morning, Scott and Carolyn called the house. Rose had been up since five that morning. The whole family came over for Christmas breakfast. Everyone opened their gifts, and Scott was having such a good time. At one point though, I looked across the room, and I could see the worry in his eyes. Everyone left after breakfast with the promise to return for three o'clock dinner.

Dinner was a joyous occasion. Everyone seemed so happy that Ed and I were home. The boys kept everyone amused with stories about Glen's new job and Scott's students. At times, it seemed so normal, I could almost forget what lay ahead. Too soon, it was time for everyone to head for home.

Scott gave me a big hug and whispered, "We're getting together with friends tomorrow, so I'll see you the next day. Are you and Dad sure you want to come with me?"

I smiled. "Of course, we are."

Ed and I fell into bed that night, totally exhausted. We were grateful for the next day's rest.

We were no longer in the melanoma department. We had moved

on to the oncology department. A new doctor reviewed Scott's chart and outlined his treatment.

"This treatment is very aggressive. It is a combination of interferon and interleukin. It's a four-month program. You will be hospitalized for one week and will need twenty-four-hour care, either by family members or private nurses. The treatment makes you feel fifty times worse than the worst flu you have ever had. We have medication for the nausea and diarrhea, but you will be very sick. After your week in the hospital, you will be allowed to go home for three weeks to recuperate. Then, you will be back for the next treatment. After four treatments, you will have surgery. There is a sixty percent chance that the cancer will not reoccur afterward."

On our drive back home, we assured Scott and Carolyn that Ed, the other family members, and I could handle the hospital care. Carolyn had enough on her hands, working part-time and caring for their four children.

Scott remained pretty quiet until he finally said, "Do you notice how my odds keep shrinking?"

FIRST WEEK
OF HELL

How do you prepare for the unknown? What do you need? What do you bring? As a parent or brother, how well would you handle watching your loved one suffer? As the patient, how much pain and suffering could you bear? I know these, and a million other questions, were spinning around our minds as Scott, Glen, and I approached the nurse's station on the first day of his new treatment.

One of the nurses led us to a large private room, showed Scott where to put his things, and told us his nurse would be with us shortly. Scott put his black gym bag in the closet and sat on the edge of the bed. He and Glen immediately began making jokes and quoting lines from movies, the silly things people say when they're nervous.

Scott finally laid back on the bed and started laughing. All he could do was point. Directly on the wall opposite the bed was a large painting of a brown wicker basket holding three fluffy white kittens with huge blue eyes staring straight at him.

"Good God, please tell me I don't have to look at them the whole time I'm in here." He laughed.

Of course, Glen thought it was hilarious and kept meowing. Soon, we were all hysterical.

At precisely that moment, Scott's nurse walked in. She looked rather confused to see the patient, to whom she was going to have to explain this most unpleasant procedure, in such a good mood. Scott immediately switched to his professional mode and introduced everyone.

"This is my first time, so I don't know how this works."

"Not to worry. I'll explain everything. In a few minutes, I'll be hooking you up to an IV. Everything is done through that so we won't be using you as a pin cushion." She smiled. "If you need nausea medication or something for diarrhea, just press this button here. Don't wait; call for medication as soon as you need it. Someone will be in as soon as possible. We try to keep you as comfortable as possible. I'm just outside. Don't hesitate to call me. If you'll get undressed, I'll be back to start your IV."

I cannot praise the nursing staff at MD Anderson enough. If ever we needed help, they responded within minutes. They were always friendly, sympathetic, efficient, and helpful. They answered every question and always explained what they were doing and why.

It soon became apparent why the patients needed additional twenty-four-hour care. Between dispensing all the medication, checking beeping machines, changing fresh linens daily, and helping patients who had accidents, the nursing staff was extremely busy their entire shift. Someone was always in and out of Scott's room, making sure everything was running smoothly.

Shortly after the medication entered Scott's system that morning, he began to feel unwell—not violently ill but definitely sick. Fortunately, a man wheeled in a large cart that contained several works of art.

"Would you like to pick out a new picture for your wall?" he asked.

Scott quickly answered in the affirmative and chose a landscape with large pine trees surrounding a deep blue lake with tall snow-capped mountains in the background. It certainly represented Scott's love of nature. Throughout the rest of the day, Scott continued to slowly deteriorate until Ed arrived to take over the night shift. Glen and I headed for the house, wondering what tomorrow would bring.

The next morning, Ed reported that the sleep medication had worked and Scott had had a good night. Soon, Scott and I were alone each day, and we settled into a daily routine. I wondered how bad the treatment would get, and every day it surpassed the last.

In the beginning, Scott could get in and out of bed with ease, but then it became more and more difficult. Almost immediately, the smell of food sickened him, yet they insisted he had to eat. There was always the hunt for food he could keep down.

By the end of the week, he was so weak, he had difficulty taking even a few steps. But he was determined not to use a bed pan, so he would struggle across the room. Every morning, no matter how hard the journey, he managed to reach the bathroom, wash his face, and brush his teeth.

During the first few days, I watched the nurses get Scott out of bed so they could change his sheets. I decided that when he was out of bed, I would do the linens and save him the hassle of a second trip across the room. I became quite adept at the job. The nurses would always say, "Oh, thank you, Mrs. Carle, but we don't mind making up the bed."

I didn't have the heart to tell them I wasn't doing it for them.

On day six, Ed headed back to Florida, as Scott was due to be released on the seventh day. On the morning of day seven, Glen and I arrived at Scott's room as they were disconnecting the interferon and interleukin.

The doctor came in early. "You will feel pretty bad today, rather like you've been run over by a truck. But the important thing is to get out of bed and walk around as much as you can. I'll be back later on today to check you out of the hospital." With that he left.

Scott immediately dragged himself out of bed, rang for the nurse, and asked if he could take a shower. She said, *yes*, as long as I stayed close by, in case he got dizzy.

Afterward, he felt so much better and began walking around the room. Slowly, as the day progressed, he began getting much stronger.

The doctor dropped by around 2:30 pm. "Well, you can't go home today because the nurses reported that you haven't been outside walking around their station. I can't let you go until we know you have your strength back."

I thought Scott and Glen were going to explode.

"You didn't say I had to walk outside. I've been walking around my room all day."

I assured him Scott had been out of bed all day.

"Well, I'll come back tonight before I go home, and if the nurses say you're doing okay, I'll sign you out."

Outside we went, around and around the nurse's station for the rest of the day. Six o'clock came and went—and then seven o'clock. Finally, Scott asked the nurse to check what time the doctor would be checking him out. We went back into his room and sat down to wait. When she entered the room, the look on her face told me the news was not good.

"I'm sorry," she said, "but the doctor already went home."

Scott wanted to go home so badly, I thought he was going to cry. I'm sure the looks on Glen's face and my own weren't much better. She left the room, and I immediately tried to soothe Scott. I told him he looked so tired; he would probably get more rest if we stayed at the hospital.

About thirty minutes later, the nurse walked back into the room and handed Scott his release papers. "I called the doctor at home. Just between you and me, I read him the riot act and got him to fax us your paperwork. I've got a wheelchair outside, and if you're ready, we can get you out of here."

The look on Scott's face was wonderful to behold. Glen ran to the elevator to go get the car, and we headed downstairs. The air was cold; it was raining, and Scott was slumped down in the chair, shivering. I finally got him settled in the backseat of the car and threw a blanket over him. I jumped into the front seat, and we headed for my house. The conversation on the way home was almost giddy, we were so happy to be out of the hospital.

At one point, Scott said, "Remember when the doctor said this would be fifty times worse than your worst flu? Boy, was he optimistic." We all laughed.

Moments later, the back of the car was quiet, and we knew Scott was asleep.

As soon as we got home, Glen headed for bed since he had work in the morning. I began getting Scott settled in the upstairs bedroom.

"Mom, I think I made a mistake. I feel terrible. I think I should have spent the night, but I just had to get out of there. Would you mind staying up here with me?"

"Of course not. I'll stay as long as you want me to. And don't feel bad; we all wanted to get out of there."

He slowly began to relax, except he kept asking me to smell his skin. He complained of a chemical odor coming off his flesh. He got up and took another shower. That seemed to help, and he finally fell asleep.

I stayed in Houston for another week while Scott recuperated, and then I flew back to Florida. Two weeks later, Ed and I were back for treatment number two.

During each hospital stay, Scott usually took his favorite pillow, blue jean quilt, portable CD player, favorite CD of a storm with rain and thunder in the background, and a few books he wanted me to read to him.

I never shared my fear of the unknown with Scott. But I remember thinking that this time we knew exactly what to bring.

Yet as the car neared MD Anderson, Scott leaned over. "Hey, Mom, people always say there's nothing worse than the unknown, but guess what."

"What?"

"Knowing is worse."

THE MAGIC KINGDOM

The interferon and interleukin treatments Scott endured over those four months seemed to be very successful. The tumor in his neck shrank significantly, and he was scheduled for another operation. They removed so much tissue that his neck looked hollowed out afterward. The biopsy of about thirty of his lymph nodes showed disease in only three. We were very encouraged.

While he was recuperating, Scott said, "When I'm better, I want to come to Florida and take Rose to Disney World."

He asked me to go to the bookstore and buy him *The Visitor's Guide to Disney World*. I would watch him sit on the couch, reading the book and making notes.

"I'll have a schedule all laid out by the time I get to Florida. We don't want to miss a thing."

The year before Rose was born, Carolyn's parents had treated Scott, Carolyn, and the three older children to a trip to Florida. We agreed to pay for their trip to St. Augustine. They had planned to drive, but after the surgery, Scott was too run-down for the trip. We couldn't afford airfare for all six of them, so Scott and Carolyn agreed that he and Rose would fly to Florida for nine days. It was 1995, and Rose would be four years old on July 23rd.

Scott finally recovered from his surgery and got a clean bill of health. The week before I left for Florida, Scott had so much fun.

Whenever we ran into a friend or relative, he'd always say, "I'm cancer-free, and I'm going to Disney World." I couldn't help but laugh each time.

They were scheduled to arrive in Florida on the Fourth of July. Driving to the airport, I was so excited; I couldn't wait to see them both, even though I had been in Houston just two weeks prior.

When Ed and I moved to St. Augustine, we had rented a two-bedroom apartment because we knew the kids would want to visit. Our three other children had visited Florida, but this was Scott's first time.

The day we went to Disney World, it was hot and humid, a typical Florida summer day. We arrived before the doors opened, and true to his word, Scott had our whole day mapped out. We spun around in a teacup until I thought I'd upchuck. We flew with Peter Pan and Dumbo and sang "It's a Small World" all day long. I had more fun watching Rose's face as we went through the Pirates of the Caribbean. She even loved The Haunted House.

We were having a wonderful time, but by six o'clock, we were talking about leaving. Just then, it began to rain. We made it to the car but decided to stop at a restaurant before going back to the hotel. Once we were in the car, Rose fell asleep in the backseat, sitting straight up wearing her Mickey Mouse ears. We found an Uno's pizza parlor just outside of the park, and Rose awoke refreshed.

We were seated out on the glass-enclosed patio. I sipped a glass of wine, Scott and Ed drank ice-cold beer, and Rose drank a mini frosted glass of root beer. We ate a delicious meal while listening to the rain pound on the glass rooftop. We were also treated to an amazing display of far-off lightning. By the time the bill arrived, the rain was just a sprinkle, and Scott surprised us by saying, "Let's go back."

"Go back?" Ed asked.

"Yeah, come on. It'll be fun. You have plastic ponchos in the car for all of us, and I bet it won't be crowded."

His enthusiasm was contagious, and Rose seemed to have gotten her second wind. As we drove down the long road toward the entrance, we were the only car on our side of the road. For miles, the exit road was jammed with cars fleeing the park. We got a parking spot right up front, and when we stepped out of the car, the storm miraculously disappeared. The air was cool and crisp with the smell of fresh rain. Once inside, we found just a handful of diehards. We basically had the whole place to ourselves.

We hit every ride we had missed and rode our favorites for a second, and sometimes a third, time. We all laughed when, at 10:50 p.m., the loud speakers announced the park would be closing in ten minutes, and Rose yelled, "What! We have to leave so soon?"

Believe me, we all slept soundly that night.

Those nine days were truly a magical time. Some mornings, I'd be up early, grab Rose, and take her on the merry-go-round at our local park. Sometimes, we'd be the only two people on the ride. We'd go around and around, staying on for two or three times and picking a new animal each time. Afterward, she'd play on the swings, and then it was off to get donuts. This gave Scott the chance to sleep as late as he liked. Some mornings, he'd get up early and take off to go fly-fishing.

Since our apartment complex was just across the street from the beach, there were lazy afternoons spent building sand castles and playing with Rose in the surf. We took a trip to the St. Augustine Outlet Mall, which had about ninety shops. Scott bought presents for Carolyn and the other children. One morning, we visited old town St. Augustine and walked in and out of buildings that were over a hundred years old. On Sunday, we attended Mass at the oldest cathedral in the United States.

We always made time for Rose and Scott to take a nap, although I felt Scott needed it more than she did. Late in the afternoon, Scott and I would sit on the couch, watching Rose play with her toys. We'd talk about his hopes that this nightmare was finally over and his plans for the future. Every night, we ate dinner in a different restaurant.

Way too soon, we were back at the airport. I stood smiling and waving until they boarded their plane that was headed back to

Houston. Even though we were scheduled to return to Texas in four days, I cried all the way back to our apartment.

When your child is battling a life-threatening illness, you wish they never had to leave your sight. You have this uncontrollable urge to clutch them in a superhuman embrace and transfer every ounce of health and strength from your body into theirs.

Rose and Scott had the same birthday, so one week later the whole family gathered for the big celebration. That summer, the film *Pocahontas* had been released. It was one of Scott's favorites. He loved the amazing animation and the music. He even tried to teach Rose some of the lyrics.

When he opened his gifts, he found one of his sisters had given him a *Pocahontas* tie and tee-shirt; the other one gave him the soundtrack from the movie. We all laughed about his *Pocahontas* birthday, but when Scott opened Glen's gift of *Pocahontas* underwear, we howled. Carolyn's family is far more serious than ours. I noticed lots of puzzled looks and shaking heads on their side of the room. Of course, our family had long since learned that not everyone appreciated our family's sense of humor.

Since my birthday was just two weeks away, I stayed in Houston until after August 5th. The kids and I had a small celebration, and then I headed back to Ed in Florida. Scott was due for his three-month checkup in October.

Throughout Scott's illness, I had kept secret my own private superstition. Scott had never gotten bad news when I was there, only when I wasn't. So I began hinting that I wanted to fly back to Houston for Scott's October doctor's appointment. Ed, unfortunately, was adamant that I should stay in Florida.

"You're exhausted. You've been flying back and forth for months. You're going home in November, and you're staying until Christmas. You need to rest."

So I stayed in Florida.

Scott's appointment was in the morning, and as the day dragged on with no call, I knew the news was bad. Finally, at five thirty in the evening, I called Scott's number. Carolyn answered.

"The new isn't good, is it?" I asked.

"No," she answered. "They found a spot on his lungs. He couldn't face calling you. He went to bed and has been sleeping all day."

"Tell him I'm fine. He can call me whenever he's ready to talk. No hurry."

I hung up the phone, threw myself into Ed's arms, and we both had a good cry. About an hour later, the phone rang; it was Scott.

"Hi, Mom. Well, we got good news and bad news. The spot is really tiny. But it's right next to my heart, so they're afraid it could spread into my heart. Great news, huh? They want to do surgery right away. You don't have to come home. You were just here."

"Don't be silly. I'll call Missy right away and check the flights. I'll be home as soon as I can."

"Thanks, Mom."

I had to admit, he sounded relieved.

I called Melissa, and she assured us a flight was available the next morning. Scott had surgery the next day. Ed stayed until Scott was released from the hospital and then headed back to Florida. I stayed until Scott had recuperated enough to go back to work. The next day, I was on a plane, headed back to Ed.

He picked me up at the airport, and as we drove back to our apartment, we both agreed it was time to go home. The next day, Ed handed in his two-week notice. After forty years of working for Grumman, he was officially retired. Soon, we were watching the moving van pull out of our driveway.

Our St. Augustine apartment was located off the coast on the peninsula of Vilano Beach. The only access to the mainland used to be across an old wooden drawbridge that spanned the intercoastal waterway. During the year and a half, we spent in St. Augustine, we had watched the construction of a brand-new giant causeway bridge. The day after the new bridge opened, Ed and I piled our suitcases into the car and drove over the new bridge for the first and last time. We were headed west, back toward Houston and an uncertain future.

HOME FOR
THE HOLIDAYS

The night we finally pulled into our driveway, all the children were at the house, awaiting our arrival. They were ecstatic that we were home for good, especially Scott. It was a workday, so they all stayed at the house as late as they could, laughing and joking.

The one emotion I began to pick up was one of immense relief. It was like their inner children were whispering, *Mommy and Daddy are home, so now everything will be okay*. I know intellectually they knew we didn't have the power to fix everything, but they couldn't help but hope. And deep down, Ed and I wished we had some magic parental powers to make Scott's cancer go away.

A few days later, the moving van arrived and unloaded the furniture we had taken to Florida. Soon the boxes were all unpacked, and the house on Swan Court was back to normal. If only our lives could have gone back to normal. We drove Scott into town for the six weeks' follow-up visit after his lung surgery, and we were very pleased when all his tests came back normal. It was time to prepare for Thanksgiving.

It was such a joyous day. The table was crowded with the entire family. I had spent three out of every four weeks in Houston once Scott's illness relapsed, but Rose had still missed me when I wasn't around. She spent the day following me everywhere I went. My mom had been so lonely while I was in Florida, she couldn't stop talking to me the whole time we were cooking our meal.

At the dinner table, everyone was so excited. The jokes seemed so much funnier, the food was exceptional, and everyone listened carefully to whoever was speaking. All our emotions seemed more intense. As the day drew to an end, no one wanted to leave. The hugs seemed stronger, and the kisses lasted longer.

The next day, once all the serving dishes had been stored away and the kitchen put back in order, it was time to move on to Christmas. Ed and I went up into the attic and began taking down Christmas boxes to decorate the house, inside and out. I also began making Christmas lists. We had a ton of shopping to do. The adults were all working and the children were still in school, so for the next two weeks, Ed and I headed to the local shopping malls.

Late one night, in early December, Scott called and asked if we could drive him to MD Anderson. He had been complaining of a painful backache, and that night he was in unbearable pain. Ed and I threw on some clothes and picked Scott up.

We got to the emergency room, and of course we had to wait. It was about one in the morning when we got in to see a doctor. He ordered a battery of tests and after several more hours, Scott was back in the ER. The doctor asked if he had done any heavy lifting.

Scott answered, "No."

I added, "Except for his four-year-old daughter."

"I'm not going to tell you not to pick up your little girl, but you probably ought to sit down before you do." The doctor smiled. "All your tests came back normal, so I think you're just doing too much. When do you see your regular doctor next?"

Scott replied that his next visit was scheduled for the week before Christmas. The doctor felt that would be fine and sent us home.

I couldn't shake the fear that visit caused. I had had a dear friend who had battled breast cancer. She had been in remission for several years and had stopped by to visit one day. She had mentioned that she had an appointment with her doctor because she had had a backache that just wouldn't go away. At her visit, she had found the cancer had reoccurred and spread to her spine. She had died a short time later. I told Ed the story, but he told me not to borrow trouble. But I couldn't shake the feeling that something was wrong.

Before we knew it, it was time to take Scott for his regular checkup. We were all so nervous because of his trip to the emergency room. Whenever he had an ache or a pain, we all worried the cancer had spread. I remember sitting in that waiting room, trying to act like everything was fine. The doctor checked Scott over and ordered a myriad of tests. We went from floor to floor, having bloodwork, an MRI, and x-rays taken. The day seemed to go on forever.

Three days later, we were back at MD Anderson waiting for the results. Scott, wearing his navy-blue down jacket, slumped down in a chair. He was leaning back with his eyes closed, trying to rest. He looked so frightened, yet he was trying to be brave. He was so much thinner than he had been less than two years ago, and his beautiful blond hair had been replaced with curly dark-brown hair that he hated. It was so hard to see him like this.

When they called his name, the four of us got up and went inside. The doctor smiled. "Well, everything looks good. Bloodwork, MRI, all normal. I guess I'll see you next year."

As we left the hospital, we were elated. "I'm going to have one hell of a Christmas," Scott said.

Scott was always off for two weeks at Christmas, just like the school kids. Every day he and the children were at our house. The kids and I made cookies while Scott and Ed worked in the shop on a beautiful carved wooden sewing box Scott was making for Carolyn. He then announced he was going on a three-day-weekend fly-fishing trip to the Guadalupe River with his two best friends, Craig and Albert.

When he came home that Monday, he was in the best mood.

"I slept better than I have in ages. Being out in the open at night, looking up at the stars, with all that fresh air, it was great. I was tired when I went to bed and slept until late in the morning, and I didn't wake up once during the night. And the fish! I caught some beauties.

We cooked them right on the fire. It was so great." It was wonderful to see the old Scott that day.

On Christmas Eve, Glenn, Scott, Carolyn, and the four children had dinner at our house. Paula and Mark were having dinner with his family in Texas City, and Melissa and A.J. were with his folks. Scott and Carolyn looked exhausted. Putting up the tree, shopping, and wrapping gifts for a large family is hard work, as Ed and I knew well. The three oldest children were excited. This was Rose's second Christmas, so she now understood the concept of Santa Claus and presents. She was practically bouncing off the walls. They stayed for a while and then left to get the kids to bed.

Christmas morning dawned bright and early. Ed and I got to work preparing the turkey for the oven. I put our traditional sweet rolls on to bake. Within the hour, Scott, Carolyn, and the four children, all dressed in their new pajamas, walked through the back door. Melissa and A.J. arrived, and my mom, Mark, Paula, and Glen got up. Christmas cookies were laid out. Soon, the gifts were flying around the room. Everyone oohed and aahed, and it looked like Christmas was a great success.

This was Glen's first Christmas since he had graduated from college. He was now working for Baylor College of Medicine in their computer department, and he decided to hand out his gifts last. We received envelopes, and we all had to open them at the same time. Inside, we were delighted to find tickets to the Broadway version of the play *Jekyll & Hyde*. It had premiered at the Alley Theater in Houston several years ago, and Ed and I had taken the family. Everyone was excited to see it again.

After all the gifts were opened and the sweet rolls and coffee consumed, everyone went home to rest. Dinner was scheduled for three o'clock.

It was another wonderful day. Everyone showed off their presents. There was so much laughter and teasing; it was such a pleasure to be surrounded by my family again. As the day wore on, I noticed that Scott looked tired. I sat next to him on the couch. "How are you feeling?"

"Oh, I'm just tired, Mom. The kids were up at five this morning, and we were at Carolyn's parents' before we came here. I'm just worn out. I think I may be catching a cold."

Soon after, they left.

For the next four days, everyone made plans for the play on December 29th. A.J. worked with a police officer who owned a limousine business, so he arranged for a limo to take them to the theater. The car held eight people, so all the kids would ride together. Ed and I drove to the theater with my mom. Melissa and Paula each brought a bottle of champagne, and off they went, laughing and joking. How I wished we could have all been together. They were so happy, and I knew they were going to have a ball.

The play was wonderful. Everyone was having such a great time. At intermission, everyone went to get a glass of wine. I decided to stay with Scott, who sat in his seat with his topcoat over his shoulders.

"Are you cold?" I asked.

"Yeah, I think I'm getting the flu. But I wouldn't have missed this for the world. Wasn't it great of Glen to think of this?"

We sat and talked about the play until everyone came back to their seats, but my heart was pounding. I was terrified this wasn't the flu.

On December 30th, we were back at MD Anderson. Scott told the doctor how he was feeling and that he thought he had the flu. They began ordering more tests. Once again, MRI, blood tests, x-rays, the whole regiment. They said that due to the New Year's holiday, it would be a few days before the results would be in.

On New Year's Eve, Ed and I spent the early evening with Scott, Carolyn, and the children. Scott still wasn't feeling well. Our other children all went out. On New Year's Day, the whole family came to the house for dinner. Scott seemed to be feeling better, but I could tell he was worried. I'm sure he could see that I was too.

On January 2nd, Scott called and asked if we would drive him and Rose over to Sam Rayburn. They had been doing major construction work on the school over the holidays, and Scott was in charge of overseeing the work. He needed to check to make sure the work would be done by time the school opened in two days.

We dropped Scott off at the school and took Rose to the nearest restaurant for some ice cream. When we returned, Scott was standing in the hall. He put his arm around my shoulders. "The doctor just called. I'm screwed, Mom. It's spread to my lungs, my spine, and my liver. I have to go say goodbye to the principal. I'll be right back."

I began to cry, and Ed asked, "Why are you crying? What did he say?"

I repeated what Scott had said. We stood in the hall, holding onto each other, crying softly, and watching Rose skip up and down the hall.

Two days later, we went with Scott and Carolyn to see the doctor. He gave us his diagnosis: Scott had three to six months to live. He brought us into a special room with padded brown-leather chairs facing a large screen. He projected the MRI results onto the screen.

I was sitting slightly behind and off to the left side of Scott. The image showed his spine, lungs, and liver. The doctor said, "The white dots are tiny tumors. You've had what's known as a disease explosion."

I watched Scott slowly slide down in his seat and lean his chin on his clasped hands.

A band tightened around my chest, and I couldn't breathe. The image looked like it had been sprinkled with snow. Ed, sitting next to me, reached across and took my hand. He squeezed it so hard, I thought my bones would shatter. I kept silently repeating, *You can't scream. You can't scream.*

LAST CHANCE

The chairs in the oncology department were upholstered in a sturdy dark-green fabric and had blond maple legs. They were relatively comfortable. They weren't the big, sink-down-into, total-body-embracing chairs of the surgery department that said, "You're here for the long haul." Nor were they the thinly upholstered seats with half-backs of the x-ray department that said, "We're the in-and-out place." Oncology chairs said, "Relax, you're probably going to be here a while."

However, in the corner of this department, over by the window, Scott had found a navy-blue chair that must have gotten lost on its way to surgery because it was way too comfortable for oncology. It was vacant this morning, and he grabbed it.

He slid down into its soft upholstery and closed his eyes. This would be our last visit to oncology. He had gotten his three-to-six-months diagnosis the day before, and although he had accepted that he was terminal, Scott was a fighter. He couldn't just go home, sit around, and wait to die. He had three young stepchildren, whom he loved like his own, and his four-year-old daughter, Rose. After he had questioned the doctor the day before about experimental drugs or new chemotherapy—basically anything he could try—his oncologist had said, "Come back tomorrow, and we'll talk."

So there we were.

I sat across from him and wondered what was racing through his mind. How could he sit there so calmly and not jump up and run around the room, screaming at the top of his lungs, like I wanted to do? Deep down, was he berating God, fate, the universe, and himself or was he composing one of his many to-do lists—what he needed to do to organize his life before his time ran out?

Soon they called his name, and we entered the doctor's office.

"There's not much left we can try, Scott, but I was at a Christmas party with a doctor who treats leukemia. We began discussing the possibility of treating melanoma with a bone marrow transplant. You would be a perfect candidate. You are strong and in perfect health, and you have three siblings."

I wanted to jump up and shout, "Are you crazy? Perfect health? Just yesterday, you told him he's going to die."

But I knew what he meant. If you looked at Scott, you would have never guessed how sick he was. He was still strong, he walked with an energetic gait, and he'd only lost about thirty pounds.

"What about his dad or me?" I asked. "We're willing to be donors."

"Sorry, parents aren't eligible. You each have only half of what he needs. We have to test all three of your children. They are all his natural siblings, right?"

Ed and I nodded.

"Good. Now you have to realize, one or more may be a perfect match, or possibly none. Go home, talk it over with the other children, and let me know. We'll have to make arrangements for them to be tested as soon as possible. It just requires a blood test, nothing painful. Years ago, they took their bone marrow to test, which was painful. Unfortunately, Scott, you'll have to go back into the hospital right away and have your bone marrow tested to make sure you are still a candidate."

Once out in the car, Scott was unsure.

"What if Melissa is the match? You know how soft-hearted she is. Remember how she wouldn't even let us kill a roach? We'd have to catch it and take it outside? What if the bone marrow doesn't take, and I die? I don't want her feeling guilty for the rest of her life."

"Scott, you know whatever happens, Dad and I will be there for Melissa. And besides, you don't know who the match will be."

"Well, I'm not worried about Glen, and Paula's pretty strong too. I know I can count on you and Dad. Do you think I should do this?"

"Son, we can't tell you what to do," Ed said. "You're the one who has to go through the pain and suffering. If you've had enough and just want to spend time with your family, then Mom and I will be there with you every step of the way. If you want to keep fighting, just say the word."

We dropped Scott and Carolyn off at their house and went home. An hour later, Scott called. "Mom, talk to the other kids, but make sure they know they don't have to do this."

First, we told Glen, and he was so excited.

"Where and when do I go to get tested? You know it's going to be me. We're both boys. We have the same genes. It better be me."

Next, we told Paula.

"Oh, thank God. We have a chance. I'm going to pray every night that it's me."

We drove over to Melissa's to tell her the news.

"Oh, thank God." She sat back, smiled this huge smile, and calmly said, "Don't worry, Mom. I know it's me. We both have the platinum-blond hair, and we look so much alike. We've always been so close. I just feel it in my bones; it's me."

Ed and I drove back home and walked into our bedroom. We sat on the bed and looked into each other's eyes. "What the hell are we going to do?" I asked.

The doctor had explained how painful the procedure was going to be. And Scott would be in isolation, all alone. What if we had a match and that child decided he or she couldn't face the pain or was afraid of the consequences down the road? We couldn't force that child to go through with the transplant. Scott would never stand for that. And how would we protect that child from the wrath of the other siblings? I have to admit, deep down we were all like Scott, thinking, *please don't let it be Melissa.* She was the most sensitive, caring, and loving member of our family—the one everyone wanted to protect.

After much thought, we devised a plan. If we had a match, we would inform that child first. If that sibling showed any hesitation, we would offer them the option of refusing the procedure. We would then tell the other children that no one was a match.

The following day, we sat in the most uncomfortable kelly-green plastic chairs at the MD Anderson lab with each of our children. I went in with the girls and watched them draw the vials of blood that held our last, desperate hope for Scott's survival. Glen worked down the block at Baylor University, so he popped in, gave his blood, and was gone.

Then came the wait.

The day the phone call came, I steeled myself for the possibility that none of my children would be a match. I was delighted, then, when the doctor said, "Good news. We have a perfect match. It's his sister, Melissa."

My reaction was twofold. "Thank God," and *Oh no, not my Melissa.* I knew how much she loved her brother, but I worried she might not have the emotional fortitude to watch her brother suffer while undergoing the procedure all alone, perhaps dying in isolation. I wondered if any of us would have the emotional fortitude needed.

When we broke the news to Missy, she immediately started crying. I began my little speech about her not having to do this if she had any doubts, but she quickly interrupted me.

"Mom, as soon as I stop crying, I'm going inside to call Scott with the good news, and then I'm going out to celebrate." She hugged and kissed us. "Go give Glen and Paula the bad news. Tell them I said, 'Ha, ha.'"

Paula started to cry. "I prayed so hard it would be me. I can't believe it's Missy. I'm next to the oldest; it should have been me. Is Melissa okay?"

"I believe so. She was going out to celebrate."

"That lucky dog." Paula smiled. "I better call Scott."

Glen, on the other hand, didn't cry; he was angry. "We are both males. It should've been me. Can I take another test? Maybe they made a mistake."

"I know you wanted to be the match, but we're just so grateful that one of you was a match, Glen."

"I know, but I love him so much, I wanted it to me. How about Missy? Is she okay?"

"Yes, she's happy she's the one. I know you wanted it to be you, honey. We all wanted to be a match, even Dad and I."

"I'm headed over to the hospital, Mom. I'll see you later."

Scott's wife, Carolyn, had been at the hospital that morning, and I was scheduled to take over. After she left, I sat down next to Scott's bed.

"I guess you talked to everybody," I said.

"Yeah. It sounded like a pretty stiff competition was going on. I'm surprised they were all so willing to do this. I'm still worried about Missy."

"She was so happy, Scott. She loves you so much; she'd do anything to help. They all would. Paula was crying because she wasn't a match, and Glen was angry."

"Well, he's still pissed. He's ready to complain to administration because they made a mistake. Don't worry; I calmed him down. I guess I never realized how much they cared."

"I don't know how come. How many people are as close with their siblings as you four are?"

"Yeah, I guess you're right."

Scott's bone marrow test came back clear, and we were ready for the transplant. But I'm not writing a fairy tale, complete with a happy ending.

The insurance company notified Carolyn that they wouldn't pay for the procedure because they deemed it experimental. Even though it was standard treatment for leukemia patients, the fact that it had never been used for melanoma disqualified it for coverage in Scott's case.

Carolyn went to war with the insurance company, spending hours on the telephone, wading through a knee-deep pile of forms, and pushing against the immovable force of bureaucracy. And while all these discussions were going on, Scott's condition slowly deteriorated.

Finally, on one sunny afternoon, we met with several doctors who announced Scott was no longer a candidate. The cancer had spread so rapidly that it was now too late.

Scott decided to try one more new chemo drug. So instead of going home, he would spend more endless days in the hospital.

THE PROMISE

Once Scott decided to try one more round of chemotherapy, I resumed my regular routine from former hospital stays.

I usually arrived in the parking hospital garage around seven in the morning, feeling a sense of urgency, and I couldn't get to his room fast enough. I'd head straight for the cafeteria and grab my first coffee of the day. Navigating the halls, corridor, and elevator, I'd gulp my drink. The slightest smell would make Scott nauseous, so I had to finish it before I entered his room.

Usually, whoever stayed the night—his dad or his brother—was waiting outside his door to fill me in. "He had a good night" was always what I looked forward to hearing. With a kiss and a hug, I'd send them off to get some sleep.

As quietly as possible, I'd slip into his room and position myself in an oversized, brown-leather chair with large wooden armrests. The foot and back of the chair could be raised and lowered to make a bed—one that more resembled the rack of the Spanish Inquisition than a real bed. I would spend the next twelve hours in and out of that chair, as needed.

The room was painted a pale, institutional gray. In addition to the chair, it contained a large hospital bed surrounded by numerous machines. The bed was flanked on both sides by nightstands, with a closet by the door. The only attempt at decoration was a large picture on the wall opposite the bed.

Every time we checked in, Scott couldn't wait to see what picture was waiting for him. Over the previous two years, there had been various baby animals, and giant floral, fruit, and vegetable still-life paintings. He was always relieved when a volunteer rolled a rack of pictures into his room and he could pick a landscape more to his liking.

No flowers or plants were allowed to soften the atmosphere because of the smell. This room had one tall window that looked out on a brick wall about three feet away. All in all, it was such an impersonal place to go about the highly personal task of dying.

Scott never brought pictures of his family to make it more personal; he said they were too painful to look at. In the past, whenever he had been hospitalized, he would bring a chain made of seven links of construction paper that he would hang on his bed. Rose would have an identical chain hanging in her bedroom. Each night, he would call her and, together, they would cut off one link of the chain. It would symbolize they were one day closer to Daddy coming home.

One afternoon, she called crying that she had cut up all the links and she wanted her Daddy to come home. Scott talked to her and gently calmed her down. When he was off the phone, he laughed. "Quick, call the doctor. I guess I have to go home now."

Unfortunately, there would be no chains this time. We had no idea when Scott would be released.

A television was mounted on the wall opposite the bed. During the day, we usually left the TV off, preferring to talk whenever he was awake. If he slept, I usually read or prayed the Rosary. But at 3:00 p.m. sharp, Scott always raised his headrest to watch his favorite show, *Batman*.

I had long ago gotten used to the constant noise of the various machines, muffled voices beyond the closed door, carts being wheeled up and down the halls, and doctors and nurses being paged on the loud speaker, as well as the competing smells of disinfectants, medications, and bodily functions. We had trained ourselves to ignore the outside world. Scott could sleep, we could talk, or I could read. We became adept at weaving our small, private cocoon, oblivious to whatever was happening elsewhere.

On one late January afternoon, Scott's favorite CD, a rainstorm, was unnecessary as wind howled between the two buildings and rain pelted the windowpane. The room's artificial light was so harsh that we always allowed the window to be our only source of illumination, so the room was dreary that day.

The first indication I had that Scott was awake was when he said, "Mom, I'm so sorry."

Rising from my chair, I stood beside the bed. "What are you sorry about?"

"All of this. Me being so sick. I know this is harder on you than anyone else."

"That's not true. You are the one who is going through all of this."

"I would have believed that if I didn't have a daughter of my own. I know that I would rather go through the fires of hell than see Rose suffer."

I assured him that I would be fine and held a straw to his chapped lips so he could drink. He seemed to drift off again, so I got a few tissues and sat back down in the chair. I turned away from the bed and dried my tears. He didn't like to see me cry.

I closed my ears to the hiss and hum of the machines and concentrated on the patter of the rain. I watched the drops slowly trickle down the pane. I was surprised when he spoke again.

"Mom, promise me you won't let this ruin your life. Life's too short to waste it."

The tears returned. The muscles in my throat constricted as I forced out the only response I could. "I'll try, sweetheart. I'll try.

A BRIGHT-
YELLOW CRAYON

Whenever Scott entered the hospital for treatment or surgery—
even that final time—within a few days, he would start
receiving mail from fellow teachers, students, friends, and family.
Soon the windowsill in his room would be covered with colorful
cards. The package he most looked forward to, however, was a large
manila envelope from the unit for students with learning disabilities.

The two teachers who ran this unit at Sam Rayburn told me that
Scott was the one assistant principal who acted as their advocate.

One of them told me, "He fought for us every year at budget
time, and he often stopped by to visit the classrooms. He'd talk to
the kids, and he loved to read their work and look at their drawings.
He was always so positive and encouraging. The students loved him."

Scott had a real interest and sympathy for students with learning
disabilities. My father, my sister, and one of my daughters struggled
with dyslexia, so he knew firsthand how difficult school could be for
these children.

We would open the envelopes, and out would tumble carefully
written cards and letters complete with wonderful drawings. I would
pull a chair up close to his bed. We would read each message and
study every drawing. Scott, being an art major, really enjoyed their
work. Some of his favorites, I remember well.

One young man's card had a drawing of a man in a hospital bed. He was obviously very ill, with IV bags hanging all around his bed. The card read, "I'm sorry you're sick. I hope you . . ." When we flipped to the inside, it said, "get well soon." There was a drawing of a man with bright-yellow hair who was definitely Scott, but he had extremely muscular arms and legs.

Scott was so tickled. "I didn't look this good before I got sick. I look like Mr. Universe."

One girl sent a sweet letter saying how much she missed him and how she was looking forward to him coming back to school. She wrote, "I know you're our assistant principal and we're supposed to hate you, but you're different. We really do like you." *Do* was underlined.

Scott laughed. "Do you think there's an unwritten rule that says they have to hate us, and nobody's told the assistant principals about it?"

Another girl wrote him a very long letter. "Mr. Carle I'm so sorry you're sick. This weekend I'm going back to my old neighborhood and I'm going to see my boyfriend. Since I moved we never get to see each other anymore so I'm very excited. We write to each other and call sometimes but we never get to see each other. We may go to the movies or maybe the park I don't know but it's okay because we'll be together. Maybe he'll kiss me. See you soon."

Scott smiled. "I'm going to talk to her teacher. I think she should get credit for this. It's a pretty decent essay."

One boy wrote a touching letter about when he first came to Rayburn. He had gotten in a fight in the cafeteria. "This big guy had me down on the ground, punching me, and you jumped over one of the cafeteria tables to stop the fight. Mr. Carle, you looked just like a superhero. I think you saved my life that day." At the corner of the letter, there was a drawing of Superhero Scott dressed in red tights with a long green cape.

Scott said this letter really touched him. "I've broken up so many fights during my career. I'm always so concerned with defusing the situation; I never thought about the poor kids who were losing."

One boy wrote a rather long letter explaining how hard life had gotten since Scott was out sick. He said everyone really missed him. "I need you to get well soon and come back to school. It's not the same when I'm sent to the principal's office with you gone. We really don't like your replacement."

Scott got a real kick out of this one. "He's one of my regulars," he said. "It's nice to know you're missed even by the discipline problems."

The best one read, "Hey, Mr. Carle, Jesus here. If you get well soon, I promise not to get sent to your office for four weeks, maybe three, and I won't wear my rosary beads around my neck for two weeks, maybe one."

"Oh, I've got to keep that one!" Scott laughed really hard. "He's one of my gang members. Don't you love the way he's hedging his bets. And he obviously forgets I already settled the rosary bead business with the gangs. The Hispanic ladies in the cafeteria got very upset. They felt rosaries were religious articles, not jewelry. I guess since I've been gone, it's started up again."

Scott was a big man, almost two hundred pounds, and had platinum-blond hair. That day, as he put the cards and letters back into the manila envelope, he smiled. "It's funny to see myself as they see me. You notice in 90 percent of them, they color my hair with a bright-yellow crayon? Not only that, in each one I look like Arnold Schwarzenegger?"

Scott understood the hard work that went into these messages. Their spelling and obvious struggle with penmanship showed the effort their cards and letters took. So after each hospital stay, when he returned to school, his first stop was to visit each classroom. He wanted to thank the students in person and talk about how much he looked forward to that manila envelope.

Scott kept that envelope in the drawer of the nightstand next to his hospital bed. Every now and then, he'd take it out and go over them. Toward the end, when he was so weak and thin, I wondered what he was thinking. I had visited Scott at the high school many times. I knew how much he loved his job, and I saw how popular he was with his students.

Could those cards, like some magic trick, transport him back to the classroom where he was everyone's favorite teacher, so tall and strong? Could he, for those few moments, escape that hospital room, and remember the life he had lived before cancer entered his life? I never asked; I didn't want to intrude. I just know that while he reviewed each one, he was smiling.

After Scott lost his battle and it was time to write thank-you letters, I returned the favor. I sent special handwritten cards to each special education class, telling those students how much Scott treasured their messages. I let them know how they had brightened his days, and I thanked them for showing him how much they cared.

VISITING HOURS

Once word got out that there would be no miracle cure, Scott was inundated with visitors: friends, fellow teachers, his students, and their parents. When visitors arrived, he always managed to sit up and was unfailingly cheerful, always joking and making them laugh.

One Saturday night, a colleague called and asked if, on Sunday afternoon, she could bring her minister by to visit. She was a member of the Antioch Baptist Church, and her minister wanted to come by and say a healing prayer. Scott said he'd love to meet her minister, and she, in turn, could meet his mom.

At one o'clock that afternoon, she knocked on the door and introduced her young minister and four ladies from the church choir. The minister was about the same age as Scott. He was holding a Bible that looked to be about a hundred years old. The black leather cover was split and cracked, the spine taped with gray duct tape. There were about fifty yellow sticky notes sticking out along the side and top of the book. The minister said a wonderful healing prayer, and he visited with Scott for several minutes.

He then introduced the ladies from the church choir and asked if they could sing for us. These ladies were plus-size women in beautiful teal-, emerald-green-, red-, and plum-colored suits. Their outfits included matching shoes and glorious hats profuse with netting, ribbon, flowers, and feathers.

They began to sing, and it was incredible. They sang three gospel hymns a cappella, and it was unbelievable. The hospital staff began to congregate around the door to Scott's room. When they finished, Scott spoke to the ladies.

"I've been singing in choirs since I was in elementary school, but we never sounded anything like you ladies. It was wonderful; thank you so much."

As the ladies left the room, they each hugged me and said they would pray for Scott.

Later that afternoon, there was a knock on the door, and an Episcopal minister walked in carrying a huge bouquet of flowers. The minister explained that his daughter was a student at Rayburn.

"She was having real problems with an ex-boyfriend. He was following her and kept calling her late at night. We went to see Scott and asked for his help. He met with the boy, and I don't know what he said, but the boy finally left her alone." He visited with Scott and also said a healing prayer for him.

After he left, I asked Scott what he had said to the boy. Scott laughed. "I asked him if he had forgotten that the girl had three older brothers who had all played on Rayburn's football team. I told him if someone was bothering my sister the way he was, I'd pay him a visit. I also counseled and sympathized with him. I said we have all had bad breakups with girlfriends and I knew he was in pain. But I told him he was young and I thought he would find another girlfriend. I guess I was right because the last time I saw him, he was with a new girl." He laughed again. "But I really think the three older brothers won my argument."

Later that day, my friend Linda Tucker arrived with her Mormon healing prayer group. They were such caring people, and they prayed over Scott and visited for a while. After they left, Linda stayed. When some of Scott's friends stopped by, Linda talked me into going down to get something to eat. I always felt guilty about how much I enjoyed those occasional breaks.

That evening, the Catholic priest assigned to MD Anderson arrived. While I waited in the lounge, he heard Scott's confession and gave him communion. Of course, by the time I came back, Scott had the priest laughing, and Father began telling us stories about his home in Ireland.

As that day drew to a close, Scott slouched down in the bed and closed his eyes. Between all the clergy and visits from friends and family, it had been a very busy day. I knew he needed to rest, so I sat in that same old brown-leather chair reading.

I have to admit, though, I was just as done in as he was. It was so hard to watch Scott bravely joke and kid with friends and coworkers, pretending he wasn't sick. The previous day, I had even asked, "If all this company is too much for you, maybe we should try to limit how many people can come to visit?"

"It's okay, Mom. They just want to say goodbye." My heart broke.

I thought Scott had finally fallen asleep when he began to talk without opening his eyes. "You know, Mom, if you could go round up a Rabbi, a Hindu priest, and a Buddhist monk, I think we will have touched all the bases today."

It's hard to explain how important those lighter moments were to me. No matter how stressful and painful those days were, Scott never lost the ability to make me laugh, and I believe sharing those laughs was just as important to him.

Early the next Sunday, I was standing by the nurse's station when I noticed a group of young people exit the elevator carrying a huge bouquet. What caught my attention were their sweatshirts: Texas A&M, University of Texas, Southern Methodist University, University of Houston, and Sam Houston State.

They headed down the hall in my direction, and I knew exactly where they were going. I hurried into Scott's room to prepare him for his visitors. I knew he'd want to be sitting up and looking as normal as possible.

I had recognized them as some of his former students. They had driven home from universities all over Texas just to say goodbye to their favorite teacher. When they walked in, Scott acted surprised. They placed the beautiful bouquet on the bureau. There were red, white, and pink flowers, with a huge yellow rose in the middle.

They grabbed chairs from wherever they could find them and surrounded his bed. They laughed about their antics in high school and their trips to Austin for the yearly conventions of TAFE (Texas Association of Future Educators). Scott peppered them with questions about their lives, steering the conversation away from himself.

"Okay," Scott said. "One at a time, what are you majoring in?"

"Finance."

"Education."

"Girls."

"Education."

"Computers."

"Education."

"Marketing."

"What's the hardest thing about being away at school?" he asked.

"Nothing."

"Math."

"My roommate."

As I stood in the corner, watching him laughing and joking with these young men and women and offering bits of advice, I realized what a great teacher he was. How they felt about him and the camaraderie they shared was so obvious.

While they were engrossed in their conversation, my mind began to wander. It was a bitter-cold February day. The rain was, once again pelting the room's small window. My eyes kept going back to the flowers and the yellow rose. It was so beautiful, yet somehow it seemed out of place.

As the visit drew to an end, Scott took charge again.

"They'll be coming in with my medicine soon, so you guys ought to take off. You'll be headed back to school before long, so go home and spend some time with your folks."

They all shook his hand. The girls looked like they wanted to kiss him but felt it wouldn't be appropriate. They filed past me, saying goodbye. The young men shook my hand, and the girls gave me hugs. But I could see the tears running down their cheeks, just like the rain on the window pane.

Afterward, Scott lay there resting. I drew a chair close to his bed and held his hand.

"They turned out just fine, didn't they, Mom?"

I whispered, "Yes, they did—and so did you."

After a while, I walked over to the flower arrangement and found a card. I opened the envelope and read the message out loud:

> Dear Mr. Carle,
> You, like the yellow rose,
> Complement all who surround you.

Scott smiled. "I bet one of the girls wrote that."

I smiled back.

"That was a really nice thing to say, wasn't it?" he asked.

"Yes. Very nice, and very true."

SHAME

The last four weeks of Scott's life were spent in the hospital. Our relationship had regressed to the way it had been during his childhood. I bathed him, fed him, and read to him. I held his hand and tried to calm his fears, even though my own fears were so strong. How could I bear to lose my son, and how could I survive his loss?

We fell into a regular routine during that time—twelve to fourteen hours together, within those four walls, until his brother or his father took over.

During the afternoon, whenever he fell into a deep sleep, I would silently slip out of his room. I'd walk up and down the halls. At times, my muscles screamed for physical activity, so these short walks were a welcome relief. I would usually stop at the nurse's station to drink a cup of coffee before returning to his room in order to avoid introducing unwanted smells into his atmosphere.

On one particular day, I threw my cup in the trash and headed back to his room. About five feet from the door, my muscles froze. I was unable to take another step. I felt as if I had waded into a field of superglue that had sealed the soles of my shoes to the ground. I bent my knees, trying to pick up my feet, but they wouldn't budge.

My mind screamed, "Oh God, I can't do this! I can't face this anymore. I can't go back into that room and watch him suffer."

Barbara Ann Carle

The flood of shame that entered my body was so overpowering, it took my breath away. How could I turn away from my beloved son, my firstborn? All his firsts had been my firsts. His first smile, his first temper tantrum, his first steps—all of them had been my first steps on my path to motherhood. I had taught him how to tie his shoes, had helped him learn to roller skate, and had typed his term papers. I had helped him live; how could I not help him die?

The shame traveled down my legs into my feet, melting the superglue. I proceeded back into his room, where I remained every day until he was gone.

It lasted just one minute—one minute out of the thirty-five years we had spent together—yet those sixty seconds have haunted me for years.

Intellectually, I know this was a normal reaction to the stress and heartache, but emotionally, it has been so hard to forgive myself.

Years later, I settled myself on the couch with a blanket and pillow—steeling myself to watch Mel Gibson's movie *The Passion*. I survived the scourging and the crown of thorns with a respectable amount of tissues. I was proud of myself; I was holding up fairly well.

Then the scene changed. Mary was rushing through the streets to get close to Jesus as He carried the cross through the city. As she drew nearer, she heard the shouts of the crowd. She stopped, turned away, and leaned against the wall. She visualized Jesus as a child—she saw Him fall, knew He was hurt, and ran to pick Him up.

Mary was brought back to the present by the jeers of the crowd. She turned and ran up to Jesus, saying, "I am here."

I drew my legs up to my chest, rested my head on my knees, and sobbed.

DNR

Her name was Anna, Mary, or Nancy. I really can't remember. She was one of the many social workers who had visited us over the almost two years that Scott had been in and out of the hospital. They were all gentle, sweet ladies, who came armed with pamphlets, booklets, and maps meant to help us navigate the giant maze known as MD Anderson. They always wore a nametag and a cheery smile. That day's lady, however, was much more somber. Her pamphlets spoke of hospice, wills, power of attorney, and DNRs.

From the beginning, Ed, Glen, and I had handled much of Scott's care. Private nursing was financially out of the question. With Carolyn working and caring for their four children, she had her hands full on the home front. She did, however, tackle the monumental mountains of paperwork, so she immediately contacted a lawyer.

The papers arrived the morning Glen, Paula, her husband, Mark, and I were headed for the hospital to relieve Ed. The Do Not Resuscitate document had to be read out loud and explained in front of two witnesses, neither of which could be members of the immediate family. I had been a legal secretary and volunteered to read the instrument.

Ed looked exhausted, so I didn't mention the papers. I knew he would have stayed if he had known, and he needed some rest. We all visited with Scott most of the morning.

Finally, I said, "I've got the paperwork for you to sign today, Scott."

"Oh, good," he replied and adjusted himself higher in the bed. I handed him the Will and Power of Attorney. He was having trouble with his vision, so Glen went over the documents with him, and he signed both.

I explained the rules for reading the Do Not Resuscitate document. Mark's friend Bobby, who Scott knew well, had agreed to be one of the witnesses, and he had just arrived. One of the nurses had agreed to be the other witness. She stepped into the room, and I began reading, trying to stay detached from the words.

Suddenly, Scott interrupted me.

"Hey, stop. I've got a question. Does this mean you guys can get tired of coming to visit me and pull the plug? I don't want you to just give up on me. I know I have lots of insurance and all."

As usual, everyone started laughing. We didn't realize the nurse had left the room until a young doctor stepped forward. "No. The question is, if you're in a coma and you're brain-dead, do you want to be kept alive even if you're basically a vegetable? Or if your heart stops and bringing you back means months more of suffering and there's no hope of you getting better, do you want to be resuscitated? Bottom line, your heart has stopped, you're gone. Do you want to come back? Do you understand?"

Scott smiled. "Yes, thank you, doctor. I do understand. No, I don't want any of those things to happen."

I lowered my eyes back to the paper. I felt my throat begin to swell, so I swallowed quickly and more often. I spread my fingers along the back side of the papers to stop them from shaking, blinked my eyes, and started reading again. My voice began to crack, and the words blurred as tears flooded my eyes. Glen stepped forward and grabbed the papers.

"Here, give me those."

I looked down at Scott, lying in the bed, trying not to laugh, and rolling his eyes. I couldn't help but smile. I grabbed some tissues and leaned into the corner of the room. Glen finished reading the document, helped Scott sign it, and passed it to the witnesses. The nurse left, and Glen put all the papers away. Then he turned to me. "Well done, Mom. I can't wait to get home and tell Dad all about this."

Of course, Scott chimed in. "Don't forget the trembling papers," he added with the appropriate hand gestures.

"And the garbled last few words no one could understand," Paula added. "Wait till Missy hears about this one."

They were all laughing and having a great time after that.

Bobby visited with Scott for a while and then walked outside with Glen and Mark. I stepped outside to also thank Bobby. Glen and Mark were in the corner holding onto each other crying, and poor Bobby was just standing there.

"Gosh," he said. "This is so strange to me. I haven't even spoken to my brother in over two years. I've never been around a family like yours. I've always liked Scott a lot, and Mark said he's been like a brother to him, but I never realized what it was like. I'm really sorry for what you guys are going through."

"Thank you. But maybe you should call your brother."

"I don't know. We don't have much in common."

There is nothing my children enjoy more than when their mother makes a fool of herself. And what a fool I was. How could I have thought I could distance myself from the words of a DNR when they related to my own son?

I have often felt that Scott and I forged a secret bargain while he was in the hospital. He would make me laugh every day, and I wouldn't cry. We both kept that bargain until that day. Yet I felt his eyes send me a silent message that said, *Mom, it's okay. You're not Superwoman.* That day I was just a mom who, try as she might, couldn't deal with the reality of losing her son.

Soon everybody left. Scott and I were alone. We didn't discuss my meltdown. We went back to our normal routine. He made me laugh; I filled him in on Rose's latest antics. We watched our 3 p.m. *Batman* cartoon. He rested. I prayed and we talked. One more precious day spent together.

FAREWELL, CHRISTOPHER ROBIN

Beep, beep, beep. The steady rhythm of the machine was muffled by the television. Scott slowly raised his bed into a sitting position. It was three o'clock in the afternoon, and no matter how sick he was, it was *Batman* time.

I pulled a straight-backed chair up beside his bed, and he began to explain what I should be seeing but wasn't. "Look at the detail in the background, Mom," he said. "The shading and crosshatching are perfect. This is the best *Batman* cartoon ever. You don't find this quality of work on many children's shows."

Watching the program through his eyes was fascinating. He explained how the artist created texture and depth in each scene. It was one of the highpoints of his day, and mine. Even though his body was ravaged by disease, his mind fought off the painkillers long enough to devour his favorite show. For that half hour, we both escaped his hospital room and journeyed to Gotham City. The Joker, Cat Woman, and Penguin flew across the screen and became not just cartoon characters but lessons in color and brushstrokes. He often chuckled and said, "Do you know how hard that is to do? These guys are geniuses."

I always called Scott my Renaissance man. He was as comfortable watching cartoons as watching *Nova*. He could as easily discuss a recent football game as the season at the Houston

Symphony. It always amazed me how much he knew about such diverse subjects. When the show was over, he lowered the bed and closed his eyes. I leaned back in my chair and closed mine.

"Glen and I had such a good time last night," Scott said. "He read me *Winnie the Pooh*. He pulled his chair right up close to the bed and laid his head on my pillow so we could look at all the artwork together. It was just like when we were kids. Remember how Glen always wanted me to read that book to him before he went to bed?"

Winnie the Pooh was special to Scott. He loved that book when he was a little boy. He often picked it as his bedtime favorite. When Scott learned to read, he enjoyed sharing it with Paula and Melissa. *Winnie the Pooh* soon became their favorite too.

But Glen loved that book. I could picture Scott at thirteen years old, sitting at the kitchen table and doing his homework. I could see three-year-old Glen, standing in his pajamas with the book in one hand and the other hand on his hip. "Come on, Scott. Read *Pooh* one more time, and I'll go to bed. I promise."

I felt my heart contract with pain. My two sons had now reversed roles: the oldest too ill to read or get out of bed, the youngest, now the caretaker, lovingly sharing their favorite bedtime story one more time.

In spite of their age difference, it's hard to describe how close those two boys had always been. Scott had written and illustrated several children's books. Since he had taught Glen how to draw, they enjoyed a special bond through children's books.

Scott was in good spirits. He was being released from the hospital the next morning. The doctor's prognosis was that he had three to six months left to live. He planned to go home and spend as much time with his family as possible. He had asked Ed and me if, as he began to deteriorate, he could move back home with us.

"I don't want to die in front of my children, Mom. They can visit every day, but I don't want them to suffer the trauma of the last months." We had all agreed this was the best course of action.

We made arrangements with the hospital for a proper hospital bed and the necessary machines to be delivered to our house. He was so anxious to get home and see his children.

"I want to get out of here. I am so sick of looking at that brick wall. I want to see trees and breathe fresh air. I can't wait to see the kids, and I know Rose really misses me."

Around five thirty, Ed arrived to spend the night. Glen and Paula walked in around six o'clock.

"Hey, Scott, we're going to take the furniture out of the family room, and I'm going to set up my bed right next to yours," Glen said. "That way I can sleep downstairs, and we can watch TV or read whenever we want."

Scott talked about the things he wanted to do when he got home. First on his list was to make a video for his family, mostly for Rose, who was only four years old.

"If I don't do this, she'll never remember me. Glen, make sure you show her pictures of me when I was healthy. I don't want her to only remember me the way I look now."

I was so unbelievably worn out that day. For the past four weeks, my schedule had been grueling. Coupled with the extreme emotional strain of helping prepare my son to die, I felt so drained. Around seven thirty, I thought Scott looked tired, so I got up out of my chair, planning to leave.

"You guys aren't leaving yet, are you?" Scott asked.

"I thought you wanted to rest," I replied, "but we'll stay if you want us to."

I really wanted to leave. I had things I needed to do at the house, and I was so weary. We still had an hour's drive home, and none of us had eaten dinner yet. But we settled back down and talked about what Scott needed us to do for his homecoming tomorrow.

At nine o'clock, Scott's eyes began to close, so we decided to leave. Everyone said good night, and I gave Scott a kiss and a hug. "I'll see you in the morning, sweetheart."

Glen, Paula, and I headed home, not knowing that tomorrow would never come.

It was cold that February night, and we were all so exhausted. We stopped at Taco Bell and grabbed something to eat. By the time we got home, I almost lacked the energy to chew. I fell into bed and was asleep almost instantly. Around midnight, I was awakened by the sound of the back door closing, and Ed tiptoed into the bedroom. I quickly turned on the light.

"Everything is fine," he said. "Carolyn showed up. Her friend agreed to spend the night with the kids so she could be with Scott. I stayed until he settled down and then came home." Ed climbed into bed, and we both had no trouble falling asleep.

At 3:45 a.m., the phone rang. Ed grabbed the receiver. "Hey. What's up? What! When?"

And I knew.

Scott had passed away in his sleep at 3:30 a.m. It sounds foolish to say we were shocked; after all, he had had a terminal disease. His last diagnosis had been for three to six months. Here it was, six weeks later, and he was gone. I felt so angry. I had counted on those few months, and I felt cheated.

I stood in the bedroom wrapped in Ed's arms, both of us sobbing. I remember repeating "No, no" over and over again. I heard footsteps on the staircase. Glen and Paula walked into the room. "What's wrong?" they asked.

"He's gone," was all I could manage.

They both sat on the floor, holding hands with tears cascading down their cheeks. Ed and I sat at the foot of our bed, and my heart broke once again as I watched his brother and sister cry. My mom was spending the night, and she slowly walked into our room. She didn't say a word, just sat down on the bed next to me and held my hand. After all, she had lost my sister eight years prior. She knew what it was like to lose a child.

By 4:30 a.m., we still hadn't notified Melissa. A.J. worked the early shift at the local Houston Police Department precinct, so we wanted to get there before he left for work. Ed, Glen, and I drove over to her house. We rang the bell and rang the bell. No answer. Glen grabbed his cell phone and called her. "Hey, Missy, answer your door. It's me."

As soon as she saw us, she knew. A.J. had gone over to work out at the tae kwon do dojo—the same dojo where Glen and Paula had become black belts. The same studio where Scott and his son Joshua had also studied. Glen went over and broke the news to A.J.

After we left Melissa and A.J.'s, we drove back home through the dark, deserted streets, and I watched pale-gray streaks of dawn light the sky. The day I had always dreaded had begun.

SORROW

The morning of February 13, 1996, I fought my way through a thick fog, trying to wake up. I knew something was terribly wrong, but I didn't know what.

In an instant, it all came crashing back. Scott was gone, and today I had to face life without him. I didn't have to rush to the hospital. I didn't have to bathe him or try to get him to eat. I didn't have to beg God to save him. It was over. The day every parent dreads had arrived. I had lost my child.

All I wanted to do was crawl back under the covers and ask God to take me too. The pain was paralyzing. How could I get out of bed, take a shower, comb my hair, cook breakfast, and pretend to some kind of normalcy when I knew nothing would ever be normal again? But I had a grieving husband and family that needed me. There were people to notify and a funeral to arrange.

As I worked around the kitchen that morning, I remember having this nagging feeling that something was physically wrong with me. My breathing wasn't right. Was I having a heart attack?

It took a moment for me to realize there was no crushing sensation in my chest. It had been there for almost two years, but that day it was gone. And it took me another minute to realize that sensation had been caused by fear. I had carried that physical manifestation for so long, I didn't even recognize it until it was gone.

Of course, the fear had been replaced by unbearable sorrow.

Sam Rayburn High School had sponsored several fund-raisers during Scott's illness to help with the medical expenses. One of those events had been selling love links. Each student could purchase a five-inch strip of red, pink, or white construction paper for ten cents. On these strips of paper, the students could write a message to Scott. The strips of paper were glued to form a circle and joined together to form a chain.

Several days before we lost Scott, one of the teachers had called Carolyn and asked if they could come to the hospital on Valentine's Day to decorate Scott's room with the love links. Since Scott was due home today, it had been agreed that the students would decorate his house instead.

When we called to notify the school of Scott's passing that morning, we had to cancel the decorations. The following day, however, the principal called to ask if they could bring the links to the funeral home. I contacted the funeral director, and he suggested they pin the links on the drapes behind the casket.

Several hours later, he called to say the students had brought so many large plastic bags of links, the links would probably pull the drapes down. He asked if they could display them in a different manner, and I said that would be fine.

We decided to help Carolyn as much as possible during this traumatic time. Ed and Glen went with her to the funeral parlor to assist her with any decisions. I took over the cooking and care of the children. Carolyn is not Catholic, so I will always be grateful to her for saying, "Mom, anything you want to do—a mass, the Rosary, anything—is fine with me."

She had the right, as his wife, to have a simple service if she chose. It was a gift to allow me to make all the arrangements and pick out the hymns and the scriptures for the mass.

The first large ordeal, of course, was the wake. When I was young, they usually lasted three days, but these days, thankfully, one night is standard.

When we arrived at the funeral home, I was shocked to see the display of love links. They had taken three six-foot tables and placed them end to end. The love links were piled about three feet high and cascaded down to the floor.

Everyone who came to the viewing asked what they were. People stood around the tables, reading the notes. "We love you, Mr. Carle," "We miss you, Mr. Carle," "Get well soon," "I promise not to be sent to your office for a month when you get back, Ha! Ha!" It was quite a sight to behold. A friend of mine called it a "waterfall of love."

The teachers from the school said there were over sixteen thousand links in the chain. That was over sixteen thousand expressions of love and caring from high school students who knew and cared for Mr. Carle.

The first thing I want to say is, we don't really know how to deal with death in our society. People feel awful, and they really don't know what to say. Inevitably, someone will say the wrong thing, but it's never with malice or to be intentionally hurtful. It's just the awkwardness most people feel around death. In addition, when we are grieving, we are not in the best frame of mind.

The one thing so many people said that bothered me was "At least you have three other children." I know what they meant; to lose an only child must be horrible. But Scott was an individual—a warm, funny, gentle man, not just a cog in a wheel. I visualized my other children holding a secret meeting, dividing him into three equal parts so they could fill the void.

One young man said, "I know exactly how you feel; my aunt died of cancer."

There was no way to explain to this childless young man that he had no idea how I felt. Losing a child cannot be compared to anything else.

Some people said, "Don't be sad; he's in a better place."

I am a religious woman; I knew he was in a better place. The problem was, I wasn't. I was stuck here on Earth trying to bury my firstborn child. As far as I was concerned, I had every right to be sad.

Every day, I had spent twelve to fourteen hours in the hospital, had come home late at night, had grabbed some fast food, and had fallen into bed. With the lack of exercise and my metabolism, I had gained a lot of weight. A friend of mine said, "Oh, I thought you would be skin and bones. I couldn't eat a thing, and I lost fifteen pounds when my daughter was sick."

That night, I sat on the side of the bed and cried. I asked Ed, "Do people think because I didn't lose weight, I didn't love him enough?"

Ed held me in his arms and whispered, "Don't let what people say upset you. Everyone knows how much you loved Scott."

Then there were all the wonderful things people said to me. One woman asked if she could speak to me in private. She stood in front of me and said, "Your child saved my child's life. My son has always been a problem at school. He goes to school, but he cuts classes; he is disruptive. We made lots of trips to the principal's office, but when we met your son Scott, he was different. He sat with my husband, my son, and me and explained how it was going to be. He said, 'I will go to every one of your classes, every day, and if you aren't in class, I will call to see if you are home sick. If you are on the campus, I will find you. I will scour the school, and believe me, I know all the hiding places. When I find you, I will take you back to your class. If you have missed too much of the work in that class and if your parents agree, you will come to my office after school. You will sit with me until you complete all your unfinished work.'

"I remember thinking, *Mr. Carle will never do that,* but let me tell you, that's exactly what he did. He checked every class, every day, and he kept my son after school every time he needed to. He wore my son down, and soon he was staying in class and getting good grades. I am so grateful to Scott. He was the first person who didn't give up on my son, and this fall, my son leaves for college thanks to Mr. Carle."

Two other parents came up to talk to me about how much Scott had helped their children with personal problems. They said his sensitivity when dealing with young adults had amazed them.

Several parents said how devastated their children had been when the announcement was made at school that Scott had lost his battle with cancer. So many people said Scott was their child's favorite teacher or assistant principal.

The ladies who worked in the cafeteria sent a beautiful flower arrangement and came to the wake. Some of them didn't speak English very well, but they took my hands and whispered, "We love him so much."

I mentioned to Glen that I was surprised the cafeteria staff seemed so fond of Scott. "He never had any money, and he usually brought his lunch in a brown bag."

"I know exactly why they liked him so much," Glen said. "I went to visit him at the school once, and he took me into the cafeteria. He introduced every one of those ladies by name, asked about their families, and checked to make sure they weren't having any problems with the students."

Rayburn's former principal, Michael Fowler, told us how good Scott had been with all the students. He assured me many of them would be at the funeral the next day, even the gang members. I remember he said, "It's easy to inspire the leaders, like the student council. But Scott even got to the gang members. They came to all the fund-raisers we had, and when I asked them why they had come, they said, 'Mr. Carle is cool.' Believe me, that's high praise from them."

I told one of the teachers how much I appreciated the "bleeding heart" flower arrangement from the student council. It was a beautiful heart-shaped arrangement of white carnations with a large, jagged strip of red flowers right down the middle of the heart. She was so relieved and said she would pass my comment on to the students.

"They wanted to spend over five hundred dollars on a giant arrangement, they were so fond of Scott. They thought the amount of money they spent on an arrangement would show how much they cared. I had to convince them that the "bleeding heart" would be better."

I made sure I sent a special thank-you note to the members of the student council.

Finally, the wake was over, and we went home. I fell into bed that night wondering how I was going to make it through the next day.

I realize a wake is an important part of grieving. It gives you a chance to see your loved ones through different eyes. I told Ed, "I always thought Scott was a great person, but that's to be expected; I'm his mother. It was wonderful to know I wasn't the only one."

I took a sleeping pill that night so I'd be sure to get some rest. Soon enough, it would be time to face the funeral.

An Altered State

I have never felt that I have psychic abilities. Over the years, I have felt Scott's presence, but only on rare occasions. However, I am blessed, or cursed as the case may be, with vivid, technicolor dreams.

The night of the wake, I collapsed into bed. Once asleep, I found myself wedged into the corner of Scott's hospital room. He was asleep, and Carolyn was seated in that large brown-leather chair next to his bed. She was reading a book, and as I watched Scott's chest rise and fall, it suddenly stopped. I lunged forward to try to resuscitate him, even though he had signed a DNR. Before I could reach his bed, Scott sat up.

The dark-brown hair that had grown in after the chemo treatment was gone. In its place, his wavy platinum-blond hair was back. He appeared to be about twenty-five years old. He stood up on the bed, and he was dressed in a light-blue button-down short-sleeve shirt, dark-navy Dockers, and brown loafers. He took several large breaths and began to jump up and down on the bed as if he were on a trampoline. He began hooting and laughing like a little boy.

After one large leap, the ceiling disappeared, and I was standing on the roof of MD Anderson. It was nighttime, cold and rainy, but I felt no chill. The surrounding Houston skyscrapers were all brightly lit. Scott jumped one last time and catapulted into the air. Arm stretched wide, he began flying through the air, zigzagging between the tall buildings. I could hear his laughter echoing through the canyons.

When he flew overhead, he shouted, "Look, Mom, I'm flying, just like my birds!"

I stood there watching him as I softly chanted, "Go, baby, go."

Watching this aerial display, what mother could wish her son back into that hospital bed to continue suffering? At that moment, I released my son. I spread my arms and ran along the rooftop, the wind ruffling my hair as I mimicked Scott's dives and turns. After one more loop around, he flew straight up into the ink-black sky. I stood watching until he disappeared from sight.

I firmly believe Scott allowed me to share the first moments of his new life. It was a gift I will cherish always.

Of course, along with the good has come the bad, and I have suffered through some terrible nightmares. I see his tall frame, gaunt and haggard. He has lived beyond his diagnosis and has come to tell me the doctors say he can't last much longer. And once again, I relive the fear and dread of what lies ahead. I often awake shattered and find those days difficult.

After Scott died, I longed for just one more moment with him; I yearned for one more hug. One night, I dreamed I saw Scott standing on a hill, holding Rose in his arms. As I walked toward him, he handed her to Glen and spread his arms. I rushed toward him and slammed into his hard, muscular chest. I felt his strong arms wrap around me. We rocked side to side, hugging and hugging. I inhaled the scent of his cologne and felt the tickle of his mustache as he kissed my forehead. At that moment, I wished never to wake up, but too soon he was gone.

In one particular dream, I was sitting on the couch in our family room. The side door opened, and in walked Scott, carrying his black leather portfolio.

"Hey, Mom, do you want to look at some of my drawings?" he asked.

We sat together and went through each one, talking about the ones I particularly liked, although in truth I loved them all. Ed walked in from the hallway and motioned me over. He leaned close and whispered, "Is he dead, or is he alive?"

"I don't know," I replied. "I'm too afraid to ask."

Back on the couch, Scott said, "Did you know that in heaven you're not allowed to draw?"

"Why not?" I asked.

"They say we're on a higher plane and that drawing is a worldly thing. I gave a speech in heaven last night stating my case as to why people should be able to draw there. It didn't go over too well." He laughed that robust laugh that I have so missed. "But don't worry, Mom. You know me; I won't give up. Tell Glen that by the time he gets here, we'll be able to draw." He leaned over and squeezed my hand. "I have to go now; they don't like it if I stay too long."

When I relayed these dreams to Glen and Melissa, they both laughed. They both had had similar dreams.

Glen had dreamed they were on the large grassy median at the University of Houston, where they had both attended college. They were racing each other across the field when Scott suddenly took flight.

"I yelled at him, 'No fair, dude! You're cheating!' And Scott just laughed. At the end of my dream, Scott said the same thing. 'They don't like it if I stay too long.'"

Melissa had dreamed of being with Scott. They were laughing and talking about their childhood together. She said he hugged her and said, "Sorry, but I have to go. They don't want me to stay too long."

I hesitate to talk about these incidents in front of Ed and Paula. Neither one has had dreams about Scott. They both feel cheated. However, they both admit they never remember their dreams. I have assured them that whenever they awake feeling particularly good, they have probably had a visitation from our beloved Scott.

Dreams can be both inspiring and devastating. Many people say it is just our subconscious mind at work. But I choose to view these visits as a gift, and I treasure the best and try to forget the worst.

I'D RATHER BE FLY-FISHING

When I read that bumper sticker on the pickup truck in the church parking lot, I didn't know whether to laugh or cry. I knew everyone there would rather have been fly-fishing—most of all, Scott.

I remembered the day, less than a year before, when he had walked through my back door. "I'm your local representative of the Make-a-Wish Foundation. For a mere fifty-dollar donation, you can grant a young boy's dying wish to take fly-fishing lessons," Scott had said in his best imitation of a TV infomercial host.

He had then handed me a flier from a local sporting-goods store, advertising an upcoming class.

"This young boy lives right here in League City. He is a husband and father of four young children. You could fulfill his lifelong wish to go fly-fishing this summer."

Of course, he had me laughing until I finally wrote out the check—a check I will always be grateful I wrote. That summer, Scott spent many peaceful hours on the Guadalupe River, doing something he really loved.

But enough of the past—the hearse was parked in front of the church, and we had a funeral to attend. Our family and Carolyn's family had arrived. All the male family members—Glen, Paula's husband, Mark, Melissa's husband, A.J., Scott's stepson, Joshua, and

137

his two best friends, Craig Dinsmore and Albert Kiecke—were pallbearers. They were all gathered in the lobby. We seated my mom, Ed's brother, and his family inside the church. Then the immediate families waited out front for the people to arrive for the service.

The funeral was originally scheduled for Thursday, but the school was having trouble arranging for substitute teachers since everyone wanted to attend. Since the students had a half-day on Friday anyway, we arranged to hold the service on that day.

I realized why the change was necessary as car after car poured into the parking lot. Students—leaning on their parents, weeping, and many wearing their Sam Rayburn letter jackets—walked by us, entering the church. Teachers, Northrop Grumman employees, Nassau Bay Police officers, and city employees—anyone who had missed the wake—stopped by to offer their condolences. I noticed the lines in front of Glen, Paula and Mark, Melissa and A.J., Carolyn, and her family were equally as long.

As the flow of mourners began to trickle down, the funeral director indicated it was time to enter the church. Carolyn with her children and sister followed the casket and pallbearers. Ed and I walked in next, arm-in-arm with the girls.

When I entered the church, I was stunned by the crowd. People were standing in the back of the church and down both sides because every seat was taken. The priest later told me it was the largest funeral the church had ever accommodated.

Since Carolyn and Scott's daughter, Sarah, is deaf, they were very active in the deaf community, so many of the mourners were hearing impaired. We also wanted twelve-year-old Sarah to understand exactly what was being said. Their friend, B.J. Janich, agreed to sign the ceremony.

I had asked if anyone in the family wanted to give a eulogy, but they had looked at me like I was crazy.

"I'm sorry, Mom," Glen said. "I just can't. I don't think I could get through it without breaking down." And I understood. Mark and A.J. volunteered to read scripture passages.

When Ed and I had met with the florist, I had said I wanted the casket covered in red roses, Scott's favorite flower. The florist had stared at me. "You want the casket covered in red roses three days after Valentine's Day?"

"Yes, I do."

"Do you know how much that's going to cost?"

"No, and I don't care."

He looked at Ed. Ed just smiled. "You heard her."

The former principal at Sam Rayburn High School, Michael Fowler, agreed to give the eulogy. It was long and quite beautiful. Unfortunately, I only remember parts of it.

"Whenever I think of Scott," he said, "the first thing I think of is laughing. He was so funny. No matter how frustrating things got at work, he always came up with some remark that made us laugh. And he was so talented. His paintings, watercolors, and pen-and-ink drawings were unbelievable. I don't know how many of you have seen the beautiful sewing box he carved for his wife, Carolyn, for Christmas. He also carved her a beautiful jewelry box. It's shaped like a tree. When you lift the lid, the limbs are compartments for earrings, rings, and necklaces. They're both truly works of art.

"Shortly after he was named assistant principal, Scott took me on a canoeing trip down Armand Bayou. I was amazed by his knowledge of flora and fauna. Plus, he could identify every bird that flew by.

"I began to wonder if someone so at home in nature could be happy in administration. Later that year, Scott turned in the most comprehensive budget I'd ever seen in my many years in high school administration.

"Scott's ability to relate to the students and interact with the parents was exceptional. As you can see from all the Sam Rayburn faces present in this church, he was truly loved and will be greatly missed."

When the service ended, we filed out of the church. The boys walked with the casket. Ed took Melissa in his arms, and I took Paula in mine. The girls were sobbing. I saw Ed's head next to Melissa's, and I was whispering to Paula, trying to soothe her while knowing there were no words that could help. Melissa later said a man she was friendly with at work had been upset that she had cried so much.

"I told him my brother was worth every tear."

Once outside, we gathered around, talking to those who had attended the service, while they loaded the casket into the hearse. As the vehicle drove down the street, I had this uncontrollable urge to run across the open field out front, shouting, "Wait, he's mine! You can't have him."

After the service, there was a huge reception in the church auditorium, so everyone moved inside. When I entered the hall, I noticed the funeral director had positioned the love links along the back wall with Scott's picture on an easel to the left and the "bleeding heart" flower arrangement to the right. A large crowd was once again gathered around, reading the notes.

So many mourners came up to Ed and me to comment on the amazing display of love from his students. The people who worked at the church said they had never seen such a unique tribute. At the reception, both families were surrounded by so many people who wanted to tell us how sorry they were and how much they loved Scott.

I was so touched when all of Scott's friends from high school and college walked in. They had driven from all over the state. We were having a reception at the house for special friends, so of course they were all invited.

At one point, while I was standing with Glen and Melissa, I said, "Wasn't it awful when the hearse pulled away?" I told them how I almost ran across the field, shouting at them to bring him back.

Glen looked so surprised, and he laughed. "I saw them drive away, and I wanted to run after them yelling, 'Hey, where do you think you're taking my brother? Bring him right back!'"

Melissa said, "I asked Dad, 'Where is he going?' and Dad said, 'It's over, honey; he's gone.' And I started crying all over again."

That was when I realized I had made a terrible mistake. No one in Ed's family or mine had ever been cremated. We went to the cemetery for a final prayer. I should have arranged for us to use one of the church alcoves for a few moments to say a final goodbye. Then we would have been prepared to see Scott taken away. Of course, when I mentioned that to Ed, he said, "Barbara, it was a beautiful ceremony; you did a great job. You couldn't be expected to think of that; I didn't."

Soon, the hall began to empty. We sent my mom and Ed's brother back to the house to set out the food while we helped straighten up the auditorium. The kids loaded all the living plants into the cars.

I asked the funeral director to pack the links in several plastic bags. I didn't know what I was going to do with them, but I knew I wanted to take them home.

All of Scott's friends were coming back to the house, so they helped transport the bags. The director handed us a box with the cards from the flower arrangements and the guest books.

Back at the house, my girls took charge. Ed and I collapsed on the family room couch. Carolyn showed up a little later with all her friends. Everyone stood around the kitchen table juggling plates heaped with ham, homemade potato salad, and coleslaw (some of Scott's favorite foods), laughing and talking. It resembled the many parties held in this house when the children were in high school and college. I kept expecting the back door to swing open, to see Scott, young and handsome, walk in holding a cold beer—for the last two years to have been some horrible nightmare. But it didn't happen.

The day finally caught up with everyone. His friends hugged me until I thought my ribs might crack, and they tried to fight back their tears as they left. Ed's brother and his family left for their hotel with plans to meet us for breakfast in the morning. My mom, Mark, and Paula were spending the night. Glen went upstairs to bed. Melissa and A.J. headed home.

I was so afraid Ed and I wouldn't be able to sleep, but we were both numb with fatigue. As I drifted off, my last thoughts focused on the next day. There was nothing left to do. All the ceremonies were over. Scott was gone, and I was now the mother of three.

Early the next morning, I decided to deal with the love links. I'd keep a plastic box of them for myself, and we'd burn the rest to be spread with Scott's ashes. I held onto that box for many years, moving it from house to house. I knew I was holding onto them for a reason; I just didn't know why yet.

Three years ago, we were moving out of our big house, headed for a high-rise in downtown Houston. Scott's daughter, Rose, then twenty-three years old, was helping me go through some of my oldest treasures.

"I have something here I know you'd like to see," I said as I slid the box off a top shelf. "These are some of the love links from your dad's funeral. You can take them and read them. If you'd like, I'd love for you to keep them."

"Oh, Grandma! I can't believe it. You have them. I've always heard about them, but no one could remember what happened to them. My mom thought they had just gotten thrown out. Of course, I want them."

That was when I knew why I had held onto them for all those years. As Rose and I stood in the room over the garage, I opened the plastic box of pink, red, and white links. I showed her the pictures of the display at the wake. We laughed and cried as I talked about how she had shown up at the reception after the funeral. She had been four and a half years old and dressed in a fancy new dress, not understanding why everyone wanted to hug and kiss her.

"You finally announced in a very loud voice that you wanted to go home. You had had enough of all these strangers touching you."

We talked about her dad, how many people loved him, and how much he loved her.

I hope those strips of construction paper will provide Rose with a link to the father she has so few memories of. Perhaps reading the messages from his students will give a glimpse of not only what kind of teacher but what kind of man he was.

THE BOOK

They say that life can turn on a dime. My ten-cent day was early that February morning when Scott lost his battle with cancer. At that moment, a door slammed shut on the happy, optimistic woman I had been, and I began the journey toward the person I am today. It was the day I was told I could no longer say, "I am the mother of four," but that I should say, "I was the mother of four." A concept I still don't accept. A mother's child is always her child, whether he's alive or not.

That day, a hole was ripped in my heart that can never be repaired or replaced. At that moment, I didn't just lose his physical being; I lost his sense of humor, his laugh, his smile, his smell, and his hugs.

Our family went from an even number to an odd. Six was a familiar number to me, a comfortable number. When I see a current picture of my family, it seems off balance.

Scott and I shared many things but especially our love of reading. At the age of twelve, he said, "Mom, I have a great book for you," and he handed me *The Hobbit*.

We shared The Lord of the Rings trilogy, chapter by chapter. Every day, he would say, "How far did you get today, Mom? What part are you up to?"

He brought me so many books. *John Carter of Mars, Dune, The Seven Chronicles of Thomas Covenant, Shogun,* and *Jurassic Park.*

I called him a book snob when he made fun of my romance novels. So much of our time together was spent sharing books.

You see, to me, Scott's life is like an unfinished book, a wonderful, fascinating, one-of-a-kind edition that I lost and can never replace. So every February 13th, I try to write another chapter.

In July 2017, Scott would have been fifty-seven years old. Would his golden hair have been sprinkled with gray, or perhaps would he have been bald? Would the laugh lines around his bright blue eyes be more pronounced? Would he have maintained his slim build or succumbed to middle-age spread?

Scott was very successful during his short life and well liked at his work place. He was only ten hours away from his doctorate when he passed away. So he would have been Dr. Carle by now. Would he have been the principal of his own school? Would he have moved into an administrative position with the district?

Would he have had more children? Would he have fallen victim to the 50-percent divorce rate? Scott was a wonderful artist. How many additional beautiful pictures would he have painted? He wrote and illustrated children's books. Would some of his books have been published?

If he had survived his illness, would it have changed him? What would he have been like if he had never gotten cancer? What would we have been like if we had never lost him?

I can't help but chronicle all the things we never got to share— watching his family grow, seeing his beautiful daughter, Rose, grow into the lovely young woman she has become.

He would have devoured the Harry Potter series. He loved Star Wars but missed the prequel. The Lord of the Rings films would have been among his favorites. I can't watch them without thinking of him. He never got to meet his namesake, his nephew Scotty.

It's been twenty-two years since we lost Scott, yet in some ways, it seems like yesterday. How often I miss hearing his voice and sharing everyday events. There are so many unfinished chapters, so many questions that will never be answered.

In *For One More Day*, Mitch Albom writes, "Every family is a ghost story. The dead sit at our tables long after they are gone." So every February 13th, melancholy floats through my door, and I play the game of "What if?"

DECISIONS

I sat on the floor, surrounded by things—ordinary items, but they weren't ordinary because they belonged to him.

I picked up his eyeglasses, and I was back in the kitchen of the house on Davon Lane. Scott came crashing through the back door, as close to tears as a fourteen-year-old boy would allow himself to be.

"Mom, Dad's going to kill me. We were playing touch football out front. I fell and bent my new glasses. I know how expensive they were. He's going to be so mad."

"Calm down," I soothed. "It was an accident. Dad will understand, and he won't get mad."

Fortunately, Dad came through for both of us. He fixed the glasses and wasn't upset. Another crisis averted.

I picked up his keys and heard his voice.

"Hey, Mom, have you seen my car keys? I left them around here someplace. Can you help me find them?"

How many times over those thirty-five years had I led the search for his disappearing keys?

"I'm going to be late for class (or work or a date)." He was careless that way.

I opened his brown leather planner and leafed through the pages. Scott died in February, so there weren't many entries. All the notations were in his neat, concise, draftsman-style printing. I came across one of his habitual to-do lists.

1. Take bird picture to be framed.
2. Turn in paperwork at the principal's office.
3. Finish latest art project.

The final line, in bold, underlined print, read, "**GET WELL.**"

What to keep? Some decisions were easy. Scott was a wonderful artist, so I kept all his paintings, drawings, sketches, the children's books he wrote and illustrated, and any articles or stories he had written.

Others were more difficult: projects he had worked on in college, assignments with special comments from a teacher. If they had been important enough for him to keep, then they were to me too. They all went into a large plastic box.

I opened a box marked "Desk Contents" that had been delivered from his office at the high school. There were pencils, pens, rubber bands, paper clips, gifts from his children, things his students had given him. I couldn't keep everything, but what if he had written with this pencil or touched this paper clip. If I threw them out, would I throw out a part of Scott?

I moved on to his clothes. I looked at his ties and could hear Glen shouting, "Hey, Scott, I got the job, but I have to wear a tie every day. I hate ties."

"No way," Scott laughed. "Ties are great. They're the only way a man can show his individuality."

I gazed at his ties and smiled. There were Bugs Bunny, Daffy Duck, St Patrick's Day, and several Christmas ties. How on earth did he even find an Easter tie? I sorted through his collection of Art Deco, Picasso and Jackson Pollack ties. He was right. They did mirror his personality.

How to deal with his clothes? Peeking out from the bottom of the pile was his brown-and-black tweed sports jacket. His dad and I bought it for him the day after he was named assistant principal. With his golden-blond hair, brown was his color. He had loved that jacket and worn it often. I decided I couldn't decide, and I carried the clothes upstairs. I hung them in an empty closet and deeply inhaled his cologne.

Glen took all his sportswear, shorts, and polo shirts. During the first year after we lost Scott, he wore them often. He said they made him feel closer to his brother. I understood.

Several weeks after the funeral, a friend gave Glen two tickets to a basketball game, and he asked his dad to go with him. It would be the first time I was alone since we lost Scott. I assured them both I'd be fine. I was reading a new book, and I planned to watch a new TV show.

"Go, have fun. I'm fine, really."

After they left, I decided to start some laundry. I picked up a shirt embroidered with "Scott Carle, Asst. Principal." I sat on the couch, clutching his shirt, and cried.

Over the years, I have slowly gone through more of his possessions. Letting go will always be hard, but it has become easier. I have learned to keep the most important things. For me, being surrounded by his paintings and pen-and-ink drawings is a comfort. I know a part of Scott still lives on in all the artwork he sold or has given away.

While we were preparing to move out of the old house, we came across his clothes.

"These are good clothes, Barbara," Ed gently said. "Someone could really use them." I knew he was right. It was time.

I agreed and off we went to Goodwill. I sat in the van and watched the workers put his clothes on the racks in the window. I saw his brown tweed jacket. I wanted to fly out of the car, run inside, and grab the jacket, shouting, "No, it's mine! You can't have it."

They say most times you think a thought, but occasionally you receive a thought. I swear that morning I heard Scott's voice say, "Mom, it's just a jacket."

I smiled. He was right. It was just a jacket. But you see, it was his jacket.

ASKING WHY

People always ask me whether I was angry after Scott passed away. I know I felt short spurts of anger, but never any long-protracted bitterness. I believe I can honestly say, "No, I never felt the deep simmering rage that some people have expressed."

I was confused, and I still don't understand why it had to happen. Maybe Ed had enough anger for both of us.

I kept thinking of the thousands of mothers all over the world who had lost their children. Why should I be any different? I consoled myself with the fact that at least I had gotten to know my son as a grown man. He had a family, was successful in his chosen career, and was a kind, compassionate individual. It must be particularly hard to lose an infant, to always wonder what they would have been like when they were grown, what path their lives might have taken.

I find great comfort in my religion. But I would often question, "Why? Why did this have to happen to Scott?"

One afternoon, I was watching television, and Rick Warren, pastor of the mega Saddleback Church in California, was speaking about the death of his son. A woman in the audience said she was unable to get over the death of her son.

"If only I knew why he had to die, I could go on."

Pastor Warren's answer was "What difference does it make?"

I was shocked by the shortness of his response. But he went on to explain. "If the Lord sat down next to you and told you exactly why He had taken your son, would you say, 'Oh, I see. That's fine'? No. There would never be a reason good enough for Him to take your son."

I couldn't help but laugh as I visualized myself standing toe-to-toe with God, arguing. Me telling Him exactly why He couldn't have Scott. No matter what He said, I'd have a clever comeback. I smiled as I pictured St. Peter dragging me away as I continued to yell exactly why God was making the biggest mistake ever.

Ed and I always go to the cemetery on the anniversary of Scott's death. We always bring ten red roses, one each for the five remaining members of our family and one each for Carolyn and their four children.

Red roses were always a family joke between Scott and Carolyn. When they had just started dating, they were out the night before Valentine's Day, and Scott had wanted to buy Carolyn a red rose. Carolyn had stated, "I don't like red roses, never have."

Scott had begun to laugh. "Oops. When you get a dozen red roses delivered tomorrow, make believe they're not from me."

Of course, after that, red roses became their flower. Carolyn carried them on their wedding day, and Scott planted red rosebushes in the backyard of every house they ever lived in.

One cold, dreary February morning, as we stood by his grave, I was suddenly seized with an almost uncontrollable wave of rage. I began pacing, crying, and railing at God. I don't remember all I said, but it was along the lines of, "Okay, I've had it! I've been a good girl. I've accepted what You sent me. I've tried to understand, but this is it." Stamping my foot, I cried, "I want him back, and I want him back right now."

I took a deep breath and looked over at an open-mouthed Ed. He began to laugh—I mean, really laugh. I was dumbfounded. How could he laugh at me at a time like this? It made me furious.

But at precisely that minute, the previous scene flashed before my eyes. The picture of me, pacing, stamping my feet, crying, and railing at God was hilarious. I sounded like a four-year-old at the doctor's office, ranting, "I didn't cry when I got my shot, so I want my lollipop, and I want it now." There I was, a grown woman, looking for a reward for surviving what God had sent me.

Ed opened his arms, and I stepped into his embrace. We stood there, laughing and crying together. As he rocked me back and forth, he whispered in my ear, "It's about time."

I've never been quick to anger, and I don't know if it's something I should have been striving for. I know that anger is a major stage in the grieving process. I don't even know if that spurt of anger was supposed to make me feel better. All I know is it made me feel as if every ounce of strength had left my body.

I guess I'd have to visit a therapist to see if my short tirade would count as one of the seven stages of grief. Perhaps I can expect a revisit of that morning's tantrum. But for now, I'll settle for my ten minutes.

ANSWERED PRAYERS

After Scott's death, sometimes during the day or night, my mind would often, suddenly, replay moments from his illness. I'd be standing at the kitchen sink, washing dishes, and in a flash, the sounds, smells, or even a full scene from his hospital room would engulf me. They wouldn't last long, but they would leave me devastated.

The one minute that seemed to reoccur most often was one day toward the end of his illness when I stood at the foot of his bed and watched Scott struggle with the neck brace he despised. Since the cancer had spread to his spine, he had to wear the brace whenever he got out of bed, and he found it unbearable.

His six-foot-two-inch frame was skin and bones, a shadow of my tall, healthy son of less than two years before. He never complained, but I could see he was pressing the morphine button more often. Earlier that afternoon, he had looked at me with little boy eyes.

"Mom, I'm so scared."

"What are you afraid of?" I asked.

"The unknown. I know I'm going to die, but what are the next few months going to be like? What if it goes to my brain, and I don't recognize anyone? What if I'm just a vegetable? What will that do to my family, to you and Dad?"

I took his hand. "We'll take it one day at a time, and one of us will always be with you. You'll never be alone. I promise."

When I found out Scott had cancer, I had immediately begun to pray as often as possible. I had begged, cajoled, pleaded, and bargained. Anything, as long as the Lord would spare my child. I had prayed for remission, an out-and-out cure, and finally a miracle.

But as the weeks dragged by and Scott's cancer progressed, his condition had gotten worse and worse. Scott was in constant pain. His lungs were failing, and he was soon on oxygen. That day, as I looked into his weary eyes, I realized we were drawing near the end of our journey.

Late that night, as I lay in bed, I knew it was time to give up. I was being selfish by holding onto him and watching him endure such suffering because I wasn't strong enough to let him go. Wanting him to survive was more about me than about him.

I told the Lord that I knew Scott was not going to survive. I prayed that He please take Scott in his sleep, not writhing in pain or gasping for breath. I remember thinking, *Thy will be done, not mine.* I fell asleep with a feeling of sadness and resignation.

Quite suddenly, Scott passed away two nights later at 3:30 a.m. It sounds crazy, but I was furious. First, with God for answering that prayer so promptly. "I didn't mean You could take him right away!" I screamed in my mind. For two years, I had prayed for his recovery, only to be disappointed time after time. But the minute I accepted Scott's fate, the Lord swooped down and took him.

Second, I was more furious with myself. Why didn't I specify a timeline? Thy will be done in two or three months. Worse, did I lose him because of my one moment of weakness, my loss of faith?

One of Scott's students had given him a book of daily scriptures, and each day we would read it. Scott and I would discuss the scripture and pray together. About a week after Scott's funeral, I remembered the book and was curious about the entry for the day he passed away. I opened it and began to cry when I read, "Thy Will Be Done."

I never told anyone about how I had given up that night. Even with that message, I still felt I was somehow at fault for Scott's death. Years later, Ed and I were having dinner with Glen and his wife, Marilyn. I began telling my story about how guilty I felt for giving up.

I was surprised when Glen started to laugh. "Oh, Mom, I stayed with Scott the Friday night before he died. He was really having difficulty getting to sleep; he was so uncomfortable. He finally said, 'I'm so tired of being sick, so tired of fighting.' I stood by his bed, held his hand, and said, 'Maybe God wants you to stop fighting. Maybe it's time to give up.' That was about 3 a.m. Saturday morning, and he died at 3:30 a.m. on Tuesday. I felt the same exact way. I didn't expect him to die so fast. I thought it was my fault. And then I didn't want to tell you what I said because I thought it would upset you. And here we are, both keeping secrets."

He came over, sat on the ottoman at my feet, and took my hand. "Mom, it was time. He was so tired, and he was suffering. We both did the right thing. We let him go. We didn't lose faith; it was a gift of love."

We all talked about how irrational death can make us. Did we truly believe that one careless word can cause someone to die? No. But it's so hard to admit that bad things happen in our lives and we are not responsible. It's almost like we look for something, anything, that we can blame ourselves for, thereby giving the illusion that we somehow have control over the tragedies we face. You look for answers to questions that have no answers in this life.

A month after his death, I began having real feelings of doubt. Did I teach Scott the right things? What if there was no God, no Heaven, and I'll never see him again? I went to church that Sunday and was surprised by the sermon. As I listened to the priest tell the story of Thomas, one of God's Apostles, who had walked with Him, talked with Him, prayed with Him, and broken bread with Him, yet doubted Jesus had risen. I realized if God could forgive Thomas, the Lord could surely forgive me. I left church that day with my faith restored.

Barbara Ann Carle

Do we ever truly accept the loss of a loved one? I doubt it. As much as my faith has sustained me through the loss of my son, I often say, when and if I make it to Heaven, the Lord and I need to have a long conversation. Because as far as I'm concerned, He has some explaining to do.

THE VIDEO

The invitation came via email—Craig Dinsmore's fiftieth birthday party. It shouldn't have come as such a surprise. Scott would have been fifty that July, but it still caught me off guard.

Albert Kiecke, Bruce Reynolds, and Craig Dinsmore had been Scott's best friends since Webster Intermediate School. They had all lived in League City, so Webster was where their paths first crossed with Scott's, and they had all become instant friends. Albert, Bruce, and Craig had been Texas State Canoe and Kayak Champions, so they had stirred Scott's interest in boating.

Every year, Armand Bayou Park sponsored a program for the blind. Canoe enthusiasts would take handicapped adults and children for boat rides on the lake. Each year, all four boys participated in this program, and it was one of Scott's favorite events.

My mom called them the ABC'S because of the first letters of their names. They remained best friends throughout college and were groomsmen in each other's weddings.

Bruce went to The University of Texas for one semester and then decided to join the Austin Fire Department. He and his wife lived in Burnet, Texas, but they still came back home for all celebrations. Scott and his friends often met in New Braunfels for fishing and camping trips. Sadly, on one of these trips, Bruce was killed in a kayaking accident at the age of thirty.

Albert also became a fireman and is now a captain with the Houston Fire Department. He and his wife divorced, but he has a lovely daughter, Amanda.

Craig married his college sweetheart, Sharon, and went to work at NASA right after graduating from Rice University.

I stood around that night listening to Scott's friends talk about their 401(k)s and retirement funds. Many had crow's feet and laugh lines, a few were graying around the temples, and some even had spreading waistlines. Soon the conversation turned to how many years they had until retirement. It was shocking to realize they were middle-aged and Scott was forever thirty-five. His career had just been starting, while theirs were now drawing to a close. It made me sad to once again realize how many years of Scott's life we had missed.

Sharon announced she had a surprise for everyone. She turned on the television, and on the screen came *The Life and Times of Craig Dinsmore to Age 30*, filmed, directed, and edited by Scott Carle. Scott and Bruce had gone all around League City filming Craig's home and elementary, intermediate, and high schools. It seemed hard to believe that Bruce had been gone shortly after the video was made.

For two summers, while the four boys were juniors and seniors in high school, they had worked for the Clear Creek Independent School District, uncrating books and delivering them to various classrooms. Of course, Scott and Bruce filmed the book depository and narrated all the crazy things they had done during those two years. Bruce even showed the two front teeth he had knocked out while using a crowbar on a wooden crate.

They talked about Mr. Stevenson, who had been overseeing their work. Scott loved to imitate poor Mr. Stevenson, who was in his seventies. He was always telling the boys, "I'll never forget my mother," and then relating stories about his youth. The first time it had happened, Scott came home laughing. "Mom, who ever forgets their mother?" he asked.

They rode over to Rice University, videotaping Craig's old dorm room, the pub where they hung out, and all their favorite restaurants.

Since Scott had attended the University of Houston and Albert was a fireman with Houston Fire Dept., the three boys had usually been together on the weekends. One semester, they even rented an apartment together in downtown Houston.

Everyone was standing around, watching the show, and laughing at the commentary, when suddenly, onto the thirty-five-inch television screen, stepped Scott. "Oh, look, it's Scott!" all his friends shouted. He stood before the camera, thirty years old, giving a monologue about the first thirty years of Craig's life. Of course, it was so funny, everyone in the room was howling.

My knees almost buckled. He looked so young, so healthy, and so alive. I had to stop myself from kneeling directly in front of the screen and having his image engulf me. My fingers yearned to brush his almost-white blond hair off his forehead, and my arms ached to embrace him once again. His essence, so real, so intense, was almost overwhelming. The sound of his voice and laughter was unbearable.

Sharon gave me a copy of the DVD. One of his friends said, "I bet you'll watch that video over and over. I know I would."

How do you explain a pain so shattering that you fear you may not survive, a longing so intense, and the realization that you can never touch your son again in this lifetime?

I put the disk in a storage bin under the television. For the last seven years, I've woken every morning and said, "Maybe I'll watch it today." After all, it's been twenty-two years; surely I'm strong enough.

I'm still not ready.

NEVER ENDING

Do not hurry
as you walk with grief
it does not help the journey.

A poem adapted from
David Elginbrod
by George MacDonald.

O ver the last twenty-two years, I have wished I could invent a
simple method to calculate the length of time one should
grieve. It would have to be direct and impersonal. Perhaps if your last
name begins with the letters A through L, you would grieve one year,
and if it begins with the letters M through Z, you would grieve a year
and a half.

Of course, no such system exists.

Grief is a journey, much like death, that we each must take alone,
no matter how many people love and support us. No one can tell you
when to start or when to stop, even though some will try.

It's been twenty-two years since Scott's death, and some people
act as if I should be over the loss. They ask, "Why are you writing
this book? Why dig up all those painful memories?"

What do they mean, "dig up"? Do they think I stuffed his life
into a few large shoeboxes and buried them in the backyard or placed

them in a local storage unit with all my unused possessions? I know exactly where these memories reside. They are seared into my brain and onto my heart. There's no searching required. Do they think I should have forgotten him by now? After giving him life and sharing thirty-five years together, should I pretend he never existed?

Some ask, "Why relive everything that happened? Why put yourself through that pain again?" which somehow implies that the pain has stopped.

After all these years, the pain is different, more bearable, but it is still there. I miss him and think about him every day.

I can see the question in their eyes. "Is she one of those women who enjoys picking at scabs?"

How do I explain that I have no choice? If sharing my experience can help one other parent deal with the loss of their child, isn't this what I must do?

I heard a minister speak recently. He said that he believed grief is tied to experience. "Suppose a five-year-old is outside playing and she is called inside. She is told her daddy is dead. The child will cry, but soon she might want to go back outside. Her experience with the father is just five years."

"His wife, however, might be overcome with grief and may think she can't go on. Her experience with the husband is far longer than the child."

"But," he said, "behold the mother. No one's grief can compare with the mother, for she has known the child since the womb."

This sermon offered me some comfort. However, I know my granddaughter Rose would disagree with his example of a five-year-old. She was four when Scott passed away, but she still feels his loss.

I had the good fortune of seeing the author Anne Lamott when she was on tour with her book *Stitches*. While she was speaking, she suddenly stopped. As an aside, she began talking about grief. I can't remember her exact words, but they were similar to this:

"We don't know how to handle grief in this country, so we have assigned time limits on it: a year for a good friend, a year and a half, or two at the most, for a parent. But I say, some grief is never-ending." I wanted to jump out of my seat and cheer.

As my good friend, Max Regan, once said, "Grief lasts as long as love lasts." To me, this is the most accurate—the true timeline. It touches my heart.

I don't believe you ever recover from the loss of a child, but I do believe you can survive. And no matter how far along you are toward survival, grief can always slip in and pay you a visit. Unexpected detours, a song on the radio, a line from an old movie, or the title of a book can catapult me back into unbearable sorrow. Even the expected events—his birthday, his wedding anniversary, and the anniversary of his death—are painful reminders of my loss. Yet each year, I somehow get stronger.

My grief is not something I wallow in. It's a private thing, a dull ache, a gnawing at my bone marrow that walks with me every day. At the same time, I enjoy my life, I laugh, and I am grateful for each day the Lord has given me. I treasure my husband, my children, and my grandchildren. I am thankful for my writing career and my many friends.

But this grief is mine, and I will take this journey on my own terms. If I want to cry, I will—no matter how many years have passed. If I want to rant and rave, it's my privilege. I've earned the right.

Just as women throughout the ages have had to claim their identity, I claim my grief. It is mine and mine alone. I will travel this path as I choose, and those who don't approve can just get out of my way.

EPILOGUE
KEEPING MY PROMISE

At some level, we understand that we will eventually lose our parents, perhaps a sibling, and someday a spouse. But we never expect to lose a child. When your son is thirty-three years old, is married, and has four children, you think he's safe. He has navigated all the minefields, and his chances of survival have increased. Then one day, he says the word *melanoma*. The bottom falls out of your life, and less than two years later, he's gone. Losing Scott has been the most painful thing that Ed and I have ever had to endure.

After Scott's death, Ed and I were numb. I would sit at the kitchen table, drink my coffee, gaze out the window, and watch spring blossom in my garden. Houston was coming back to life, but inside I was dead. Often Ed and I would sit, paralyzed, on the couch and stare into space. I would have been content to hide from the world forever.

Often, I fantasized what it would be like to spend one more day, one more hour, with Scott. What would I do? What would I say? I knew all the things I wished I had said when he was alive.

But one day, I began to wonder what he would say to me. Would he hold my hand and calmly whisper, "Mom, I know how much you loved me, and I understand why you sit, staring into space"?

Barbara Ann Carle

I knew my son better than that. During those last weeks, we talked many times about what he wanted his dad and me to do when he was gone. And doing nothing was not one of the choices.

I could almost hear his voice. "Mom, get off that couch and start living. Don't waste the gift God has given you. Remember your promise."

My first challenge was Ed. He is a master carpenter, builds beautiful furniture, and can do amazing home improvement projects. One morning, as we were sitting at the breakfast table, I looked up at the light fixture. "I've never liked that thing. Do you think we could replace it?" I saw the first spark of interest in his eyes that I'd seen in ages.

"Sure," he said. "Let's go look for one this afternoon."

After the new light was installed, I kept coming up with small projects, and soon he was back working in his shop. I then encouraged him to return to his retirement club meeting.

We both joined the local gym. Ed walked on the treadmill while I took a water aerobics class. I met several funny, interesting women, who still remain dear friends.

I decided I needed to try something new. I'd always been interested in cake decorating, so I took a class. One class turned into three. I began turning out wonderful confectionary delights. But I started to lose control of my weight, so I began giving the cakes away.

The one thing that kept us going after losing Scott was our grandchildren. We decided to spend more time with them. After Scott had passed away, Carolyn enrolled in school, so we offered to babysit four-year-old Rose during the week. She also stayed with us during the summers when Carolyn eventually went to work. When Rose started school, her classmates became the recipients of my specialty holiday cakes. We attended every one of her Grandparents Days and all her school events.

In 1998, Paula gave birth to a beautiful baby boy, whom she named Scotty. She and Mark were living in Corpus Christi at the time. Soon, Ed and I were on the road twice a month to visit our new

grandson. In the summer, Rose would often join us on these
journeys.

While keeping up with all our other grandchildren—Joshua,
Sarah, Emily, Rose, and Melissa and A.J.'s son, Adam—and their
many activities, Ed and I led a full and busy life.

One Christmas, Glen's wife, Marilyn, recommended a writing
class taught at the Spectrum Center in Houston. I was welcomed into
a circle of unbelievably talented writers who became treasured
friends. I was amazed at the comfort and relief I found by putting my
thoughts and emotions down on paper. Writing became my outlet.
Essay by essay, poem by poem, some funny and some sad, I slowly
worked my way through great portions of my grief. As my body of
work grew, my writing teacher encouraged me to share it with others.

I began reading at area venues. At first, I limited them to
humorous essays. My work was well received, and as my confidence
increased, I decided to share some serious pieces about Scott. Rather
than lose audience members, the line of people who stayed to speak
with me after the readings grew. Many were parents who wished to
talk to me about the loss of their children. And they asked where they
could read more of my work. I began submitting essays, which were
published in anthologies, magazines, and several Chicken Soup
books. This book has been a ten-year work of love that I hope will
help some of those parents.

I read an announcement that the Poet Laureate of Texas was
speaking at a local bookstore. That night, I met an amazing group of
poets who invited me to join the local poetry society. I began
attending meetings and taking classes. Eventually, I submitted my
poems to magazines and anthologies. I was pleasantly surprised at
how many were accepted for publication.

In 2009, my first poetry book, *New York Rhapsody*, was released.
In the summer of 2017, my second book, a collection of poems
about Scott entitled *Cave Drawings*, was published.

Scott fought his cancer with a bravery and a sense of humor that
made his story worth telling. Through this series of essays and the
collection of poems, I introduce the reader to a young man who

faced death with faith, laughter, and great dignity. For as long as people read my words, his story will continue.

None of this happened overnight; it took years. It was a slow, painful process. And we had our setbacks. One year after we lost Scott, Ed had a nonmalignant tumor removed from his brainstem. Six years later, he had open heart surgery. Fourteen years ago, I lost my mother. But once you've practiced the "one foot in front of the other" philosophy long enough, it becomes habit. Even on the hardest days, I've had that conversation from that rainy January day at MD Anderson to fall back on. Scott so badly wanted me not to throw my life away on grief.

I often wonder, would I have been so open to expanding my life if it weren't for that promise?

But life, to Scott, never meant sadness and depression. It meant joy and delight. He made me laugh almost every day of my life. So I vowed to laugh and to make at least one person smile every day. I don't just live my life, I enjoy it; I embrace it and all that comes my way. I know he would approve.

I was Scott's mother. I know he had faults and made mistakes, just like any other human being. For close to two years, while I sat by his side watching his unfailing struggle to live, he never complained, he never gave in to anger or bitterness, he never lost his faith, and he always maintained his amazing sense of humor. As far as I'm concerned, while I know he wasn't a saint, he came darn close.

I marvel at Scott's generous spirit. He spent his last days preparing his loved ones for the future. He not only encouraged us to go on with our lives but gave us the permission to be happy. Scott gently nudged each of us down the path he wanted us to travel. And that is a gift all of us will always cherish.

MELANOMA

For centuries, pale alabaster skin was considered the epitome of female beauty. During the Victorian Era, a white complexion was so valued, ladies would bleach their skin with lemon or dandelion juice. Some even went so far as to use creams mixed with arsenic or mercury, which often proved to be fatal.

Women's daytime fashion was designed to protect their bodies from the sun, featuring high collars and long sleeves. When going outside, ladies wore large hats, or sunbonnets and gloves, and they carried parasols. Pale skin was considered a sign of refinement and class distinction for both sexes. Only men who worked as laborers or women who could not afford domestic help were exposed to the sun and had tanned skin. White skin indicated the ability to spend extended time indoors.

For a short time in the 1900s, lying in the sun was believed to be a cure for tuberculosis, but that never proved to be successful.

It wasn't until 1923 that, according to legend, famed fashion icon Coca Chanel was accidently sunburned while sailing on the Riviera. When she arrived back in Paris with a golden tan, women believed this was a new beauty trend and immediately began to tan their skin. It was also the Roaring Twenties, and women began to wear less restrictive clothing (shorter skirts and sleeveless tops). They were more active outdoors. Suntans were said to give ladies a glowing, healthier-looking complexion.

This attitude persisted until the late 1990s, when researchers found that 90 percent of skin cancer was caused by exposure to the sun's ultraviolet (UV) rays.

The most serious type of skin cancer, according to the Mayo Clinic, is melanoma. It develops in the melanocytes, which are the cells that produce melanin—the pigment that gives skin its color. Melanoma can also form in the eyes and, though rarely, in the internal organs, such as the intestines.

Barbara Ann Carle

The exact cause of all melanomas isn't clear, but exposure to UV radiation from sunlight or tanning lamps and beds increases the risk of developing melanoma.

The risk of melanoma seems to be increasing in people under the age of forty, especially in women. Knowing the warning signs of skin cancer can help ensure that cancerous changes are detected and treated before the cancer spreads. Melanoma can be treated successfully if it is detected early.

Factors that may increase your risk of melanoma include:

- Fair skin.
- A history of sunburns.
- Excessive UV light exposure: sun, tanning lights and beds.
- Living closer to the equator or at a higher elevation.
- Having over fifty moles or having unusual larger-than-normal moles or ones with irregular borders or a mixture of colors.
- A family history of melanoma.
- Weakened immune system, such as in people who have undergone organ transplants.

The American Cancer Society predicts that about 91,270 new cases of invasive melanoma will be diagnosed in the United States in 2018. Of those diagnosed, about 9,320 are expected to die—about 5,990 of which are estimated to be men and 3,330 of which to be women. Members of my family avoid the sun as much as possible and visit our dermatologists every six months. We try to follow as many of the Melanoma Prevention Guidelines, listed on the next page, as we can. It sounds like a lot of work, but believe me, after losing Scott, the precautions are worth it.

Barbara Ann Carle

MELANOMA PREVENTION GUIDELINES

- **Seek the shade**—Especially between 10 a.m. and 4 p.m.
- **Do not burn.**
- **Avoid tanning** and never use UV tanning beds.
- **Cover up** with clothing, including broad-brimmed hats and UV-blocking sunglasses.
- **Use a broad-spectrum (UVA/UVB) sunscreen** with an SPF of 15 or higher every day. For extended outdoor activity, use a water-resistant, broad-spectrum (UVA/UVB) sunscreen with an SPF of 30 or higher.
- **Apply one ounce** (two tablespoons) of sunscreen to your entire body thirty minutes before going outside. Reapply every two hours or immediately after swimming or excessive sweating.
- **Keep newborns out of the sun.** Sunscreen should be used on babies over the age of six months.
- **Examine your skin** head to toe every month.
- **See your physician every year** for a professional skin exam.

Additional information about melanoma is available from the American Cancer Society, MD Anderson, and the Mayo Clinic websites.

ACKNOWLEDGMENTS

I never set out to write this book. One Christmas, my daughter-in-law said, "Have you ever thought of taking writing lessons?" She told me about a creative writing teacher, Max Regan, who came from Boulder, Colorado, to the Spectrum Center in Houston once a month. She said everyone raved about his classes, so I signed up. I have been attending those classes ever since. I began writing essay after essay, and over the last fourteen years, I have amassed a body of work that resulted in this book.

Most people assume a writer sits alone in his or her study, pen or pencil in hand, and whips out a first draft that becomes a book. Oh, how I wish that were true. This book was exceptionally painful to write, and there were times I got too depressed to continue. It was at these moments that my fellow writers, friends, and family stepped forward to encourage and comfort me.

Every book comes to fruition with the aid of a team of supporters. Over these many years, my team leader, Max Regan, became my mentor and dear friend. He inspired me to tell the story of Scott's brave battle with illness. He never let me give up, and he never lost faith in me.

I owe a great debt of gratitude to the amazing writers in the monthly Spectrum Center Writer's Guild's Staying Serious group. Rosa Glenn Reilly, Melina Miller, Ellen Seaton, Diana Galindo, Kirsten Cerre, and Ron Bueker supported me with thoughtful suggestions and their gentle, helpful critiques.

Many thanks go out to my peer readers, who helped shape this book: Kay Cox, Roger Roffman, Carol Wolf, Pam Brown, and Barbara Ragland. Also to my friends—Susan Gordon, Lisa Fierer, Diana Dettling Buckley, and Ruthie Stevenson—my proofreader, Becky Newberry, and my copy editor and formatter, Dorothy Tinker.

I also want to send my appreciation to the many members of Max's Ten-Day Writing Project Retreats in Boulder, Colorado. Whenever I attend, I return to Houston enriched by your talent.

I would also like to send my sincere thanks to the doctors, nurses, and staff of MD Anderson Cancer Center for the wonderful care, comfort, and treatment they provided Scott during his illness. The assistance and support they offered our family during this painful ordeal will always be remembered and appreciated.

Of course, none of this would have been possible without the love and support of my husband, Ed. He lived every moment of this book by my side. He held me up when I thought I couldn't take another step and has been my strength. Our three children, Paula, Melissa, and Glen, traveled this journey along with us, and they are always a source of love and inspiration.

I also want to recognize my daughter-in-law Carolyn Carle, who was widowed at such a young age. She went on to build a new life as a single working mother, raising four young children. She has amazingly devoted her professional career to assisting families of terminally ill patients arrange for hospice care.

Finally, I have been blessed with the love of my six wonderful grandchildren: Joshua Haise, Emily Haise, Sarah Haise, Adam Van Dorn, and my small but devoted fan club, Rose Carle and Scotty McDaniel.

ABOUT THE AUTHOR

Barbara Ann Carle is an essayist, poet, and novelist.

Barbara's essays have been published in numerous anthologies, including *Thanksgiving to Christmas*, a *Patchwork of Stories*, *That Thing We Do*, *Fearless Nest*, and five Chicken Soup books: *The Chocolate Lover's Soul, Democrat's Soul, Republican's Soul, Grieving and Recovery*, and *It's Christmas*.

Her poems have appeared in various publications, including the 2009 Poetry Society of Texas's *A Book of the Year*, where her poem "The Battle" won the Ted O. Badger Award, the 2011, 2012, and 2013 Texas Poetry Calendars, the 2012 Summer Edition of *Rattle Magazine*, and the 2016 Mutabilis Press anthology *Untameable City*.

Barbara has written two poetry books. *New York Rhapsody*, a collection of poems about growing up in New York City before and right after World War II, was published in 2009. *Cave Drawings*, a selection of poems about her son, Scott, was published in 2017.

She is a member of the Spectrum Center's Writer's Guild, Gulf Coast Poets, The Poetry Society of Texas, The Divas of the Written Word, and Women in the Visual and Literary Arts.

Barbara was born and raised in New York City but has been a Texas transplant since 1965. She is the mother of four and the grandmother of six. Barbara presently lives in a high-rise in downtown Houston with her husband, Ed. She is presently at work on a new novel.

www.ingramcontent.com/pod-product-compliance
Lightning Source LLC
Chambersburg, PA
CBHW051831090426
42736CB00011B/1748